MIMESIS
INTERNATIONAL

LITERATURE

n. 13

T0279189

ANDREA COMININI

PETER CHURCHILL

The Forgotten Novels of a British Secret Agent

Preface by David Stafford

MIMESIS
INTERNATIONAL

© 2022 – Mimesis International
www.mimesisinternational.com
e-mail: info@mimesisinternational.com

Isbn: 9788869773983
Book series: *Literature* n. 13

© MIM Edizioni Srl
P.I. C.F. 02419370305

INDEX

This book is dedicated to
Simon Churchill, an authentic friend

DAVID STAFFORD
PREFACE

Peter Churchill was one of the most celebrated British secret agents of the Second World War. He was one of the first recruits of the Special Operations Executive (SOE) and undertook three secret missions into occupied France, but during the fourth one was captured by the Abwehr and spent the rest of the war in various Nazi prisons including several months solitary confinement in one of the worst of the concentration camps, Sachsenhausen. His female courier, Odette Sansom, who was captured alongside him, barely survived a regime of torture in Ravensbruck. He was no relation to British Prime Minister Winston Churchill. But he and Odette convinced the Germans that he was, and this undoubtedly saved their lives. At the end of the war Odette was awarded the George Cross (and the first woman to receive this prestigious award), and Churchill the Distinguished Service Order (DSO) and the Croix de Guerre. They married in 1947, and three years later the film Odette, starring leading British film stars Trevor Howard and Anna Neagle, transformed them into national celebrities. Subsequently Churchill wrote three books drawing directly on his personal wartime experience: *Of Their Own Choice* (1952), *Duel of Wits*, (1953), and *The Spirit in The Cage* (1954). A fourth book, the novel *By Moonlight*, (1958), he set against the background of the *maquis* uprising on the Glières plateau in the French Alps.

These books are the focus of Andrea Cominini's absorbing study. Churchill died in 1972, long before the concept of intertextuality became commonplace amongst literary scholars. Yet he would certainly have accepted the idea, demonstrated convincingly by the author, that his writings were influenced by, and freely borrowed

from, other literary works and genres. Born in Amsterdam as the son
of a British Consul, he had a peripatetic upbringing, read Modern
Languages at the University of Cambridge, was bilingual in French
and fluent in Italian, and Spanish. Through a careful analysis of each
of his books, Cominini shows how much Churchill's knowledge
of literature influenced his writing, including his almost poetic
descriptions of characters, his skilful use of dialogue, humour, and
sarcasm, as well as his references to other authors dealing with the
kind of trauma he suffered during his long months of isolation in
Sachsenhausen. He was also clearly familiar with the world of film,
and in places his writing is highly cinematographic. His books freely
cross the boundaries between memoir, autobiography, and war and
spy novels. The first two, for example, are written entirely in the
third person with only a single clue that the protagonist is Churchill
himself. Only in *The Spirit of the Cage* does he frankly reveal his
actual identity and develop the plot in the first person. Creative
non-fiction novels is perhaps the term that best describes them.
These, in the author's words, 'are narratives characterized by the
depiction of actual contemporary events and real historical figures
using the styles and techniques of fictional discourse that provide an
immersive context in which the narration of actual events is as lively
as the presentation of fictional worlds.'

Yet the question of whether Churchill's books are 'true' is more
than a literary one. When Professor M. R. D. Foot published his
official history of SOE in France in 1966, Churchill sued him for
implying that he and Odette had mostly led a luxurious life in the
south of France at SOE's expense. The case was settled out of court,
the offending passages were deleted, and the book's first edition
was withdrawn from circulation. What Foot actually wrote about
their activities within SOE's SPINDLE and CARTE networks was
undoubtedly barbed. 'Luxury, in the end, was as much a cause of
SPINDLE's undoing as were the stresses in CARTE. [Churchill and
Sansom] found that life could still be easy for people with plenty
of money on the Riviera,' he wrote. 'Consequently they fell out
with some of their subordinates. After the war, floods of favourable
publicity and strong counter-currents of hostile gossip washed
around this unfortunate couple, who then married and were later

divorced. The truth is that the military value of their mission was slight, though this was not wholly their own fault.'

Foot was a professional and scrupulous historian. What lay behind his doubts about Churchill's exploits? It seems clear that in part this was due to the fictionalized versions that Churchill had produced in his books, not to mention the film Odette and the book on which that was based. In his bibliography to SOE in France, Foot described Churchill's first three books as no more than 'reasonably accurate,' while he dismissed the Odette biography as 'a popular and partly fictionalized life' that was only 'accurate in parts' - comments that survived the libel suit into the second edition. Foot, who died in 2012, never explained why he was so skeptical. Yet as late as 2004, in his entry on Churchill for the *Oxford Dictionary of National Biography*, he noted dismissively that his subject had written 'three light-hearted books' about his wartime adventures.

Cominini's book, with its emphasis on intertextuality, provides a valuable service in helping us understand how Peter Churchill became the celebrity that he did, and hence the focus of such impassioned controversy. His personal file is now available for public scrutiny in the British National Archives, and Cominini has drawn upon it to provide some valuable biographical information. Furthermore, he adds a fascinating and hitherto overlooked dimension to Churchill's life as one of three extraordinary brothers as well as to the family that nurtured them. The eldest son, Walter, was an ace Spitfire pilot awarded both the DSO and DFC who was in charge of Malta's air defences and was killed in August 1942 while leading a raid on Sicily. The youngest, Oliver, also served with SOE. After being awarded the Military Cross for an operation on Corfu, he was parachuted into Northern Italy in 1944 as liaison officer to General Raffaele Cadorna, military commander of the partisans, and later survived several perilous weeks in German-occupied Milan. Indeed, it was Cominini's exploration of this mission, which he outlines in some detail, that eventually led him to discover Peter Churchill himself. Like his two brothers, Peter was a man of enormous courage and resourcefulness and his books, however we classify them, are far from light-hearted as claimed by Foot and provide an authentic mirror of the everyday life of a British secret agent during the Second

World War. They have been largely and undeservedly forgotten. Andrea Cominini is to be thanked profoundly for reminding us of their significant literary interest and historical value, as well as for documenting the extraordinary contribution of an English family at war.

David Stafford is the author of several books about SOE, including the official British history Mission Accomplished: SOE and Italy 1943-1945, (The Bodley Head, 2011), as well as a history of the spy novel, The Silent Game: the real world of imaginary spies. (Viking, 1988). His latest book is Oblivion or Glory: 1921 and the Making of Winston Churchill, published by Yale University Press in 2019. He is a professor emeritus at the University of Edinburgh and currently lives in British Columbia, Canada.

PART ONE

RESEARCH

During the summer of 2010, I was leafing through an old tiny book called: *La neve cade sui monti* by Vitale Bonettini,[1] partisan member of the group C3 of the Fiamme Verdi[2] in Valle Camonica in 1944. Between the lines I was attracted, taken by surprise, by the presence of an important foreign surname: Churchill. This wasn't definitely my first reading of the little booklet, written as a diary, because Bonettini was born and grown up in my own village Esine. In the short chapter titled «Al nuovo accampamento» (At the new campsite), a few lines introduced and described a mysterious Major parachuted in the area and named Churchill:

> One beautiful day Captain Sandro arrives with a man called Mr. Antonio. I notice that he shouldn't be one of us, he is well groomed and too clean. Somebody says he is an English Major.[3]

Who was this baffling *Mr. Antonio*? In the short footnote about him Bonettini wrote: «The English Major Peter Churchill». A name and a surname. I began researching immediately, thinking that finding his identity would not have been too strenuous, but the destiny was playing me a dirty trick. After having contacted, with no results, some still-living partisans quoted by Bonettini in his book, I tried

---

1   Bonettini Vitale (*Tani*), Esine (1926 - 1994).
2   The *Brigate Fiamme Verdi* (Green Flame Brigade) was an Italian Partisan Resistance Group, of predominantly Roman Catholic orientation, which operated in Italy during World War II.
3   "Un bel giorno arriva il capitano Sandro, con un tale che si fa chiamare signor *Antonio*. Si vede che non è dei nostri, è troppo tirato a lucido. Si mormora che sia un maggiore inglese" *Tani* Bonettini, *La neve cade sui monti - Dal diario di un ribelle*, El Caròbe, Esine, 1975, p. 36 [in the text my translation].

a quick research on the Web. In just a few minutes I succeeded in finding a certain Peter Churchill, an Englishman who had taken part in World War II, enlisted in the SOE (*Special Operation Executive*).[4] According to the first information I got, he had accomplished some secret missions as a parachutist secret agent and, very important detail, seemed to have operated mainly in France, but also in the North of Italy, albeit not in 1944 but in 1945, and not in Valle Camonica but on the Alps of Trento.

Naively I thought I had reached my goal and I began focusing on the figure of this Churchill. He turned out to be a Captain and not a Major as stated by Bonettini, but this, in my opinion, was only an insignificant detail. Maybe Bonettini, very young at the time he wrote his diary, confused the military ranks. About the incongruity of the years and the places, not very far between them, I overlooked them and, so caught up in the excitement, I was gently carried by the fulfilling sensation of having found out something never unveiled before and that, for so many years, had been hidden between the lines of a dusty old war diary. Satisfied by the short but productive research, for a while I abandoned the issue.

Only later I reconsidered some inconsistencies arisen during my research and which were instilling in me a more and more uncomfortable sense of doubt. So, I decided to restart my research, beginning from all the details collected before and trying to clarify once and for all the true identity of Peter Churchill. After having

---

4   The Special Operations Executive (SOE) was a British World War II organization. It was officially formed on 22nd July 1940 under Minister of Economic Warfare Hugh Dalton, from the amalgamation of three existing secret organizations. Its purpose was to conduct espionage, sabotage and reconnaissance in occupied Europe (and later, also in occupied Southeast Asia) against the Axis powers, and to aid local resistance movements. SOE operated in all territories occupied or attacked by the Axis forces, except where demarcation lines were agreed with Britain's principal Allies (the United States and the Soviet Union). It also made use of neutral territory on occasion, or made plans and preparations in case neutral countries were attacked by the Axis. The organization directly employed or controlled more than 13,000 people, about 3,200 of whom were women. After the war, the organization was officially dissolved on 15th January 1946.

contacted the *National Archives* of Kew (UK),[5] I got really good news. Just one year before, after 64 years since the end of World War II, most of the files and documents concerning the operations of SOE during World War II had been declassified and so they were available to the public. I was able to get in touch with an archivist[6] who immediately helped me. She confirmed very soon that the Peter Churchill I found was not the right person I was looking for. He was a parachutist, a secret agent member of the SOE, and he was really a Captain and not a Major, and yes, he operated on the Alps, but not in Valle Camonica and not in 1944.

At that point I was afflicted but, not long after that, I received an email from the same archivist. Following my request, she examined in depth my research and discovered that Captain Peter Churchill had two brothers, one an officer and pilot in the Royal Air Force,[7] and the other a secret agent in the SOE, with Major rank. Moreover, the latter was parachuted in Valle Camonica during the summer of 1944. After having received all the documents and files requested, I identified the real Churchill who met Bonettini: William Oliver Churchill, brother of Peter.[8] All the confusion arisen around his name

---

5   *The National Archives (TNA)* is a non-ministerial government department. Its parent department is the Department for Culture, Media and Sport of the United Kingdom of Great Britain and Northern Ireland. It is the official archive of the UK government and for England and Wales. The National Archives is based in Kew in the London Borough of Richmond upon Thames in south-west London.

6   M. Spire Rosalie, archivist in The National Archives (TNA), Kew (UK).

7   Churchill Walter Myers (24/11/1907 - 27/10/1942), aeronautic engineer, pilot and Captain of the Royal Air Force during the WWII. He was the eldest of the three Churchill brothers and was a pilot since 1932. He took part to the famous Battle of Britain, against German Luftwaffe and he was killed in action while leading a raid in a Spitfire on Biscari airfield near Gela in southern Sicily on 27th August 1942. He was buried at the Syracuse War Cemetery.

8   Churchill William Oliver was born in Stockholm in 1914 and educated at Stowe School and Cambridge University where he read Modern Languages at King's College, after which he studied architecture at Cambridge before his studies were interrupted by the war. He soon became a Special Operations Executive (SOE) officer and in September 1943 he was parachuted into German occupied Corfu to inform the Italian commander that the Allies would support him. In August 1944, he was parachuted into northern Italy behind German lines to act as British Liaison Officer with the partisan leaders. It is here where he met the partisan Bonettini. After the war, he married Ruth

was due to his battle name. In fact, Oliver, for his mission in Valle Camonica in the summer of 1944, was named as *Anthony Peters*. Probably Bonettini mixed up his poor information or, maybe, the same Oliver gave his real surname, just to make his figure more mysterious, adding it to his battle name. In that way, Major William Oliver Churchill, with his battle name *Anthony Peters*, claimed to be a man called *Antonio* pretending to be Peter Churchill in real life. But the astonishing thing is that a real Peter Churchill, his brother, truly existed at that time, and was also an SOE agent. To confuse the already complicated situation of the identities even more, the real Peter Churchill, during his missions for the SOE, used, among others, *Pierre Olivier* as name of battle, the French version of his brother's name. Summing up, Major Oliver used the surname *Peters*, while his brother, Captain Peter, used the surname *Olivier*. This expedient was probably very useful and sure during the dangerous moments in enemy territories, when one has to be always ready and plausible in producing his own personal information. The name of the respective brother, indeed, would have been remembered easily and with a certain resolution, so as to avoid any suspect from the interlocutor.

From that point on, everything was easier. After further online research, I succeeded in finding one of the sons[9] of Oliver Churchill who, henceforth, gave me many files, documents and material about the Churchill brothers and later became a really good friend of mine. In April 2015, I presented a historic essay about the Major Oliver Churchill and his mission in Camonica Valley in 1944 during an international historic convention at the Università Cattolica del Sacro Cuore of Brescia and later, in June 2018, the essay was published.[10] Only from that point on I decided to research, deepen and analyse the figure of his brother, Captain Peter Churchill. Surprisingly, I

Briggs, who, together with the famous mathematician Alan Turing, was a key member of the British Intelligence code-breaking team at Bletchley Park during the war. They moved back to Cambridge where Oliver practiced as an architect. He died in Cambridge in 1997.
9   Churchill Simon, born in Cambridge in 1949.
10   Cominini Andrea, "La missione alleata Fairway: Un Churchill in Valle Camonica", in *Gli Alleati a Brescia tra guerra e ricostruzione - Fonti, ricerche, interpretazioni*, edited by Rolando Anni, Giovanni Gregorini, Maria Paola Pasini, FrancoAngeli Edizioni, Milano, 2018, pp. 135-154.

discovered that not long after the war he became a writer, a novelist precisely, and that, thanks to his books, he gained celebrity all over the World for a short period of time,[11] but suddenly disappeared and nobody remembers anything about him anymore.

---

11   Peter Churchill actually wrote five books: *Of Their Own Choice*, Hodder and Stoughton, London, 1952, *Duel of Wits,* Hodder and Stoughton, London, 1953, *The Spirit in the Cage,* Hodder and Stoughton, London, 1954, *By Moonlight*, Robert Hale Limited, London, 1958, about the period of WWII and only later he wrote a sort of tourist's guide entitled *All About the French Riviera*, Vista Books, 1960.

PART TWO

PETER CHURCHILL
A Biographical Note

2.1 *Early life*

Peter Morland Churchill[1] was born in Amsterdam on 19th January 1909, the son of the British Consul William Algernon Churchill. He had a peripatetic upbringing as his father's postings subsequently took him to Pará in Brazil, Stockholm, Milan, Palermo, and Algiers. His father was also an art historian and he was the author of what is still the standard reference work on early European paper and papermaking.[2] Peter was educated at Malvern School from 1923 to 1927, then spent 18 months at Chillon Castle and Geneva University in Geneva. He was very clever and had a good propensity for languages, which brought him to the University of Cambridge, where he read Modern Languages at Caius College. Moreover, Peter had the opportunity to grow bilingual in French and could speak fluently Italian and Spanish, thanks also to his continuous wandering. He came from a wealthy middle-class family and he had two brothers, Walter, born in 1907 and Oliver, born in 1914.

1   *The National Archives*, Kew (UK) - Ref. HS 9/314 - HS 9/315 (Personal Files Peter Morland Churchill), 1939-1946.
2   Churchill William Algernon, *Watermarks in paper in Holland, England, France, etc. in the XVII and XVIII centuries and their interconnection*, De Graaf, 1935. William was the son of Henry Adrian Churchill who was an archaeologist.

2.2 *Sport achievements*

During his years in Cambridge, he became famous also in sports, where he excelled. Peter was proficient at exhibition diving, a first-class skier, and played golf off a six handicap,[3] but he was especially excellent in ice-hockey, being considered the finest ice-hockey player the university had produced.[4] It is believed that the three Churchill brothers, Walter, Peter, and Oliver were encouraged to take up ice-skating by their mother, who was a proficient figure skater.[5] Peter played in the Varsity matches gaining many blues,[6] and also in European matches, captaining the Cambridge University team in his final year, and winning 15 international caps. He played in the England team during the Ice Hockey European Championship in 1932 in Berlin, where England ranked 6th.

2.3 *Job career*

After his school and sport careers, in 1932Peter became a publicity agent for hotel advertising magazines in Lausanne and between 1934 and 1936 he moved into the British diplomatic service, working as British Vice-Consul in the Netherlands before and after working as Pro-Consul in Oran, Algeria. In 1936, for only one year, Churchill worked in a cycle factory in Birmingham and, from September 1937 until the summer of 1939, he became a sport news reporter and subsequently worked in a fur business. Finally, from September 1939 to August 1940, he was Under Secretary to Sir

---

3   *The National Archives*, Kew (UK) - Ref. HS 9/314 - HS 9/315 (Personal Files Peter Morland Churchill), 1939-1946.
4   Marks Leo, *Between Silk and Cyanide: A Code Maker's War 1941-45*, published September 12th 2000 by Free Press, first published 1998.
5   This and other following personal information have been given to me by Simon Churchill, son of Oliver Churchill, Peter's brother.
6   A "blue" is an award earned by athletes at a university and some schools for competition at the highest level. The awarding of blues began at Oxford and Cambridge universities in England.

Norman Birkett in the Home Office Advisory Committee, and later became President of the Committee.[7]

2.4 *Secret Agent during WWII*

At the outbreak of the Second World War, Peter Churchill was commissioned into the Intelligence Corps and also underwent commando training. In April 1941 he joined the Special Operations Executive as one of its early recruits and was assigned to the French Section in June 1941.[8] His nom de guerre were *Michel, Raoul* and *Pierre Olivier*. His undercover identities were *Pierre Chauvet* and *Pierre Chabrun*. He was infiltrated into France four times, for four war missions as SOE agent, twice by submarine and twice by aircraft, and spent 225 days behind enemy lines.[9]

2.5 *Operation Willow*

In late December 1941 he sailed in Polish liner SS Battory from Glasgow to Gibraltar where he transferred to submarine depot ship HMS Maidstone. En route to the Côte d'Azur, he transferred to submarine P36 which took him 2 miles offshore Miramar (Théoule-sur-Mer), west of Cannes, on 1st January 1942. His first secret mission, called *Operation Willow*, had just begun. His duty was to inspect three SOE networks in the south of France, evaluate their strengths and weaknesses, assess their needs, and give them instructions. He was also given two million francs (equivalent to approximately £480,000 / €500,000 in 2022) to distribute between the three networks, one million for their sustenance and the other one

---

7   *The National Archives*, Kew (UK) - Ref. HS 9/314 - HS 9/315 (Personal Files Peter Morland Churchill), 1939-1946.
8   Here is a short report on his training activities done in July 1941:
     Was best at Morse test. Good at all subjects. Still shows plenty of interest and is extremely interested in demolitions. Doing very well at Morse. The National Archives, Kew (UK) - Ref. HS 9/314 - HS 9/315 (Personal Files Peter Morland Churchill), 1939-1946.
9   Churchill Peter, *The Spirit in the Cage*, Hodder and Stoughton, London, 1954.

destined for the release of ten French patriots from Fort St. Nicholas prison in Marseille. After having completed his mission, Churchill then planned his return to England. Together with some friends and a guide he travelled by train to Perpignan and then crossed the Pyrenees on foot walking about 80 km to Bañolas near Figueras. He then reached the British Consulate in Barcelona and soon after that he was driven to Gibraltar, passing through the Spanish border hidden in the trunk of the car. On 14th February 1942, Peter was flown back to London for debriefing and, before his successive mission, he was promoted to Captain.

2.6 *Operation Delay II*

His second mission, called *Operation Delay II*, was actually a brief expedition to deliver four SOE agents by submarine to the French Riviera. On 26th February 1942, Peter flew from Bristol to Gibraltar with two radio operators. In Gibraltar they were joined by another radio operator and an SOE agent. After that, they travelled in HM Submarine P 42 "Unbroken" to Antibes where on the night of 21st April 1942 Peter went by canoe to the shore with two of the radio operators and their radios. He led them to a secure house and then he returned to the submarine. Successively, the same night, the other SOE agent and his radio operator were dropped off by canoe too at the Pointe d'Agay and Peter came back once more to the submarine, which then sailed for the Italian coast.[10] So, also his second mission was accomplished and, on his return to England, Churchill was given his next mission by his Headquarters.

2.7 *Back to England*

His next job would have been very dangerous and Peter needed a long training before going through it. Together with other two

---

10   Mars Alastair, *Unbroken. The True Story of a Submarine,* Pan Books, London, 1954.

French agents, he should have been parachuted south of Paris, at Sainte Assise, near Fontainebleau, where they had to blow up a powerful radio transmitter which the Nazis were using to direct their U-boat campaign, and which was so powerful that the U-boats could pick up its messages without having to surface. But before he and his two French helpers could undertake the mission, a failed attempt by another French agent to attack the same powerful radio station resulted in significantly increased security around that area and Churchill's mission was called off. This unexpected fact brought Churchill and his headquarters to change their mind and plan something different. In the following days, Peter asked for some action and soon after, his third mission was ready.

2.8 *Third Mission*

On 27th August 1942, Peter was parachuted near Montpellier and went to Cannes to organize and coordinate the SOE "F" Section "Spindle" Network which directed the delivery of supplies to support the Carte Organization run by André Girard, *Carte*.[11] Moreover, Peter had to act as liaison officer between Carte Organisation and the SOE Headquarter in London. Among the couriers at his disposal, Churchill had Odette Sansom, *Lise*,[12] with whom he was to develop a close relationship, and his wireless operator was Adolphe Rabinovitch, *Arnaud*.[13] This task was very different from the previous missions he had accomplished: it was something concerning organisation and planning, which should have been updated day by day, depending on the external situation. It surely was not a clear mission with an

11   Girard André (25 May 1901, Chinon, Indre-et-Loire - 2 September 1968, United States of America) was a French painter, poster-maker and Resistance worker. During the Second World War he founded and headed the CARTE network, also taking "Carte" as his personal codename.
12   Sansom Hallowes Odette (28 April 1912 - 13 March 1995), also known as Odette Sansom and Odette Churchill, was an Allied intelligence officer during the Second World War.
13   Rabinovitch Adolphe (27 May 1918 - 1944), also known as Alec Rabinovitch, was a Special Operations Executive officer in France during the Second World War. He rose to the rank of captain.

exact goal, but rather something on the field, changing and evolving every day.

Soon after his arrival in Cannes, Peter learned that Francis Basin,[14] another SOE agent who was head of the Urchin network on the Côte d'Azur, had been arrested in Cannes on 18th August and so he planned to rescue him when he was being transferred by train to Lyon, but this attempt was called off, apparently at Basin's request.[15] It was during this period that Churchill arranged an arms drop for General de Lattre de Tassigny,[16] Commander of one of the sole French Divisions still in existence, based in Montpellier.

Several attempts were made by the Headquarter to fly Churchill back to the UK. The first attempt was for a Hudson bomber to land at Vinon near Aix-en-Provence to collect him as well as *Carte* and five French generals. However, the landing field had not been measured properly by the French Resistance and the runway proved to be inadequate, so Churchill aborted the landing. The second attempt was from Arles, in late December 1942, amid the presence of German troops, but also this one was unsuccessful. The third attempt was on a small abandoned airfield near Tournus between Mâcon and Chalon-sur-Saône in January 1943. The Germans had covered the planned landing strip in piles of bricks to prevent a landing and these had to be cleared quickly. The Hudson bomber landed but got stuck in heavy mud and had to be towed out by horses. The plane brought 10 men and collected 10 others, but Churchill was not one of them. It turned out that some of De Gaulle's agents had planned landing at the same time.[17]

Meanwhile, on 8th November 1942, Hitler ordered the occupation of the southern zone of France, in reaction to the landing of the Allies

---

14   Basin Francis (1903 -1975) was a French secret agent of the *Special Operations Executive* too.

15   Foot Michael Richard Daniell, *SOE in France. An Account of the Work of the British Special Operations Executive in France 1940-1944,* London: H. M. Stationery Office, 1966.

16   De Lattre de Tassigny Jean Joseph Marie Gabriel (2 February 1889 - 11 January 1952) was a French military commander in World War II and the First Indochina War.

17   All this information, and the following, about this mission, are collected from: Peter Churchill, *Duel of Wits,* Hodder and Stoughton, London, 1953.

in North Africa, and as a result André Girard moved his "Carte" operations from Cannes to Arles. Churchill was then advised that two police inspectors had called at his accommodation in Cannes searching for him, and so he too had to change lodgings immediately. In November 1942, one of Girard's couriers (André Marsac) was travelling by train from Marseille to Paris carrying a list of names and addresses of hundreds of potential Carte members, and while he was sleeping, an Abwehr[18] agent stole his briefcase containing the important list. The next day Marsac was arrested in Paris by Abwehr intelligence officer 'Colonel Henri' Hugo Bleicher[19] who put him in Fresnes prison.[20] Bleicher convinced Marsac that he was an anti-Nazi German officer and could help release him from Fresnes prison and in this way he succeeded in contacting other agents (among them also Odette) and in collecting a lot of information about the rest of the resistance group, evaluating it and noting its inadequate security measures.

In the meantime, Churchill was instructed to arrange a further attempt for a Lysander[21] to land at Basillac near Périgueux. The Lysander arrived at the scheduled time but did not respond to Churchill's signaling and departed, only to return shortly after. The landing had to be aborted when it was clear that the Germans had anticipated it, and Churchill and friends had to escape on foot and hide. Peter and Odette left Périgueux quickly by train to Toulouse where they found a safe house. Here the couple was informed that all passengers on an earlier train from Périgueux had been met by the Gestapo and questioned, and that Peter's flat in Cannes has

---

18 The Abwehr was the German military intelligence service for the Reichswehr and Wehrmacht from 1920 to 1945.
19 Bleicher Hugo Ernst (9 August 1899 - August 1982) was a senior non-commissioned officer of Nazi Germany's Abwehr who worked against French Resistance in German-occupied France.
20 Kramer Rita, *Flames in the Field: The Story of Four SOE Agents in Occupied France*, Michael Joseph Ltd, 1995.Fresnes Prison (*Centre pénitentiaire de Fresnes*) is nowadays the second largest prison in France, located in the town of Fresnes, Val-de-Marne South of Paris. During World War II, Fresnes prison was used by the Germans to house captured British SOE agents and members of the French Resistance.
21 The Westland Lysander is a British Army co-operation and liaison aircraft used immediately before and during the Second World War.

been raided, people had been arrested and others had departed. So, Churchill decided it was too dangerous to remain in Cannes and relocated all the Spindle network to Saint-Jorioz on Lake Annecy in Haute-Savoie, and changed his cover name from *Pierre Chauvet* to *Pierre Chabrun*. Here he arranged for arms to be supplied to the Maquis des Glières.[22]

London arranged further attempts to land a Lysander and only on the night of 22/23 March 1943, at Estrées St. Denis near Compiègne, one of them successfully collected Churchill, while Francis Cammaerts, nom de guerre *Roger*,[23] took over the Spindle network in his absence.[24] Moreover, the Headquarter of SOE in London was suspicious of 'Colonel Henri' and, when Churchill came back to the UK, they instructed him that on his return to France he was to make no contact with him, and to avoid Odette until she had broken links with him.[25]

2.9 *Fourth Mission*

On 15th April 1943, after only three weeks in the UK, Peter was ready for his new and fourth mission. He was parachuted back onto the mountains above Saint-Jorioz on the banks of Lake Annecy, one more time in France territory. Here he met Odette but both were arrested later in the day in St. Jorioz by Hugo Bleicher of Abwehr. Churchill and Sansom claimed they were a married couple and related to the British Prime Minister Winston Churchill, just to be seen as more valuable prisoners and less likely to be executed as

---

22   The Maquis des Glières was a Free French Resistance group, which fought
     against the 1940-1944 German occupation of France in World War II. The
     name is also given to the military conflict that opposed Resistance fighters
     to German, Vichy and Milice forces.
23   Cammaerts Francis Charles Albert (16 June 1916 - 3 July 2006) was a Special
     Operations Executive (SOE) agent who, together with peter Churchill and
     others, organised French Resistance groups to sabotage German
     communications in occupied France.
24   Marks L., *Between Silk and Cyanide: A Code Maker's War 1941-45*, cit.
25   Foot, *SOE in France. An Account of the Work of the British Special Operations
     Executive in France 1940-1944*, cit.

spies.[26] The Germans believed them and lately they were sent to different concentration camps. Here they were sentenced to death but, thanks also to the false kin with Winston Churchill, both escaped execution. So Odette was transferred to the concentration camp in Ravensbrück, where she endured terrible torture, but revealed nothing to her captors.[27] Peter was initially taken under Italian custody to the barracks in Annecy, where he was badly beaten after an unsuccessful escape attempt during which he assaulted an Italian guard. He was then transferred to German custody and moved to Fresnes near Paris where he was questioned by Bleicher. On 13th February 1944 he was transferred to Berlin for more questioning and on 2nd May, Churchill was sent to Sonderlager "A" Sachsenhausen, where he was held in confinement for 318 days. Finally, on 1st April 1945, he was moved by train to Flossenbürg in Germany, fifty miles south-east of Bayreuth, where he was held for four days before being taken by truck on a 30-hour trip to Dachau where, rather than being taken to the notorious concentration camp,[28] he was lodged in a former brothel along with other officers. As an officer, he was given better treatment than most of the 22,000 inmates of Flossenbürg,

---

26   Letters at the Winston Churchill Archives Centre reveal that in the autumn of 1944 General Redman, deputy commander of the French Forces of the Interior, contacted Downing Street to ask whether Peter Churchill was indeed a relation. Private Secretary Jock Colville replied that if Peter was a relation he was a very distant one. (In his 1947 letter to WSC, Peter would estimate that they were 62nd cousins). Correspondence, General Redman and WSC's private office, Churchill Papers, CHAR 20/142B/155-57.

27   Odette remained in the concentration camp at Ravensbrück, where she spent the rest of the war, part of it in solitary confinement, part of it in the commandant's quarters. She saved her life mainly thanks to two lies, that she was married to Peter, and that her husband was Winston Churchill's cousin, and these allowed her to have alleviation among the horrors of the concentration camp. When the American Army got near the camp in April 1945, she was finally liberated. After a brief rest in hospital, she was reunited with her three daughters. *The National Archives*, Kew (UK) - Ref. HS 9/648/4 (Personal Files Odette Marie Celine Hallowes, nee Brailly, aka Odette Sansom, aka Odette Churchill), 1939-1946.

28   Dachau Concentration Camp was the first of the Nazi concentration camps opened in Germany, intended to hold political prisoners. It is located on the grounds of an abandoned munitions factory northeast of the medieval town of Dachau, about 16 km (10 mi) northwest of Munich in the state of Bavaria, in southern Germany.

who were forcibly evacuated on the 200 km death march to Dachau Concentration Camp, during which one third died.[29] The following day, as the Americans were approaching Dachau, Peter and 30 other officers were taken by bus to Innsbruck, where he was held in the local Straflager (punishment camp). He then was joined by 140 other high profile prisoners, generals, politicians, royalty, German anti–Nazis and other Prominenten (notable prisoners), including former Austrian Chancellor, Dr. Kurt von Schuschnigg.[30] On 24th April 1945, together with them, Churchill was taken by SS guards from Dachau over the Brenner Pass to a village called Villabassa (Niederdorf the Tyrol).The purpose of this transfer, ordered by the Obergruppenführer of SS Ernst Kaltenbrunner,[31] was to deliver these important prisoners to the Anglo-Americans, in exchange for his safety but, when the Allied troops reached the small village on 28th April, negotiations failed. The SS guards in the transport had orders to kill everyone if liberation by the advancing Western Allies became imminent. However, when they reached South Tyrol, regular German troops of Wehrmacht took the inmates into protective custody.[32] Meanwhile, all the prisoners were stuck in a remote hotel on the shores of Pragser Wildsee (Braies Lake), where on 5th May they were finally liberated by the American 42nd

---

29   Cziborra Pascal, KZ Wolkenburg: *Todesmarsch nach Dachau* (Die Außenlager des KZ Flossenbürg), Lorbeer-Verlag, June 2018.

30   Richardi Hans-Günter, *Ostaggi delle SS al lago di Braies - la deportazione in Alto Adige di illustri prigionieri dei lager nazisti provenienti da 17 paesi europei*, Braies, Archivio di Storia Contemporanea, 2006. Together with Peter there was many others important personalities from 17 different countries, between them the Prime Minister of the Third French Republic, Léon Blum, the son of the famous Italian Marshal Badoglio, Mario, and some relatives of the Count Claus von Stauffenberg, who played a key role in the unsuccessful assassination attempt to Hitler on 20th July 1944 and who was later executed for this reason.

31   The Obergruppenführer of SS Ernst Kaltenbrunner was the highest-ranking member of the SS to face trial at the first Nuremberg trials. He was found guilty of war crimes and crimes against humanity and executed on 16th October 1946 by hanging.

32   Richardi, *Ostaggi delle SS al lago di Braies - la deportazione in Alto Adige di illustri prigionieri dei lager nazisti provenienti da 17 paesi europei,* cit.

Infantry Division and the 45th Infantry Division.[33] The following days, Churchill was taken to Naples for debriefing by officers from the Crimes Investigations Departments and testified against his former captors. On 12th May 1945, Churchill was flown back to England.[34] The war was finally over.

2.10 *After the War: Honours, Marriage, and Literature*

Figure 1. Peter and Odette in 1949
(photo donated by Peter to his brother Oliver on 25 January 1950).

---

33   In 2015, the documentary/fiction *Wir Geiseln der SS,* directed by Christian Frey, was produced. In the documentary is shown and described the arrival and the following liberation of the prisoners stuck in Villabassa and later at the Pregser Wildsee Hotel.

34   All this detailed information about Peter Churchill and his participation to the war as a secret agent were taken from his personal files at *The National Archives*, Kew (UK) - Ref. HS 9/314 - HS 9/315 (Personal Files Peter Morland Churchill), 1939-1946.

After the war, Peter was awarded the Distinguished Service Order (DSO) and the Croix de Guerre,[35] and in 1947 he married Odette, his trustworthy courier who accompanied and helped him during his third and fourth missions in France and shared with him the long captivity.[36] Their public profile was supported by Jerrard

---

35   Maj. Gen. Sir Colin McVean Gubbins, who was the prime mover of the Special Operations Executive (SOE) in the Second World War, wrote the Recommendation for DSO for him:
     This officer carried out four clandestine missions into France between the end of 1941 and the spring of 1943. He was first landed by submarine in the south of France in December 1941 with the mission of contacting the principal organizers in the unoccupied zone, to bring them directives, remedy their various difficulties, improve communications and arrange help for arrested members of the organization. This involved much travel and dangerous liaisons activity, but CHURCHILL carried out the mission with complete success and return to England in early February 1942.
     His second mission was to organize the infiltration of a number of agents by sea into the South of France. Although this involved a short stay in France, it was nevertheless a delicate and hazardous task. It was mainly due to CHURCHILL's courage and resourcefulness that the operation was successfully carried out.
     In April 1942, he was parachuted into France as chief liaison officer to a large resistance group in the south. He worked here for several months organizing parachute dropping operations and the reception of agents by sea on the Mediterranean coast. His operations were always well organized and he took great personal risks to ensure the safe disposal of infiltrated agents. In March 1943, Capt. Churchill paid a short visit to England for consultation. Two months after his return to France in May 1943, he was arrested. By that time, he had decentralized the organization to such an extent that his work could be continued by others. He was released by Allied troops in Germany in May 1945.
     Capt. Churchill worked tirelessly and unselfishly over a long period in very trying conditions, showing outstanding courage, leadership and organizing ability, which earned him the respect and admiration of all who came in contact with him. It is strongly recommended that he is appointed a Companion in the Distinguished Service Order. The National Archives, Kew (UK) - Ref. HS 9/314 - HS 9/315 (Personal Files Peter Morland Churchill), 1939-1946.

36   Also Odette, after the war, was awarded the George Cross (she was the first woman to be awarded it ever), 1939-1945 Star, France and Germany Star, War Medal 1939-1945, Queen Elizabeth II Coronation Medal, Queen Elizabeth II Silver Jubilee Medal, Légion d'honneur (Chevalier), Order of the British Empire (Military Division) (Member). Escott, Beryl (2012). *The Heroines of SOE: F Section: Britain's Secret Women in France.* Stroud, UK: The History Press. Two short movies, taken at the same moment, exist in the British Pathé Archive (Film ID: 2158.11, Canister: UN 1695 B and FILM ID:

Tickell's biography of Odette in 1949,[37] a non-fiction novel based on her wartime experience, and followed a year later by Herbert Wilcox's film adaptation *Odette*, starring Anna Neagle as Odette and Trevor Howard as Peter Churchill. This film had a huge resonance in the United Kingdom, so much that King George VI and his wife Queen Elizabeth Angela Marguerite Bowes-Lyon attended the premiere on 6th June 1950.[38] Shortly afterwards, Churchill began publishing his wartime memoirs, in three volumes: *Of Their Own Choice* (1952), *Duel of Wits* (1953) and *The Spirit in the Cage* (1954). Although he had been surely a good secret agent during the war period, criticism of his SOE career persisted after the war and, especially following the release of the film *Odette* (in which he played a cameo role). Several former resisters, including Francis Basin and André Girard,[39] both Churchill's war partners, publicly attacked him and Odette, questioning their right to be portrayed as heroes of the Resistance. Probably, some of this indignation was motivated by jealousy and bad blood, but this fact scratched Peter and Odette's reputations. Moreover, in 1966, the publication of M.R.D. Foot's official government history, *SOE in France. An Account of the Work of the British Special Operations Executive in France 1940–1944*,[40] revived the controversy: in reviewing their efforts, Foot suggested that Churchill and Odette had lived a life of luxury

---

VLVA9T4MBIQ6RD0E8F2NBSKMRVTLB - FILM ID: N/A). They show Peter and Odette outside the Kensington Registry Office at 28, Marloes Road, London, after their civic marriage ceremony.

37 Tickell Jerrard, *Odette: the story of a British agent*, Chapman & Hall, London (UK), 1949.
The figure of Odette was further studied and described recently in the book of Larry Loftis, *Code Name: Lise: The True Story of the Woman Who Became WWII's Most Highly Decorated Spy*, Gallery Books, 15th January, 2019.

38 Film ID: 2302.05, Canister: UN 2264 A and Film ID: 2302.06, Canister: UN 2264 B, British Pathé Archive.

39 Francis Basin and André Girard both collaborated with Peter Churchill during his third war's mission in France.

40 Foot, *SOE in France. An Account of the Work of the British Special Operations Executive* in France 1940-*1944*, cit.
Michael Richard Daniell Foot, (14 December 1919 - 18 February 2012), known as M. R. D. Foot, was a British military historian and former British Army Intelligence Officer and special operations operative during the Second World War.

on SOE's money and had accomplished little of military value. Only in 1968, Churchill accepted a settlement and a full apology, and the text of later editions of *SOE in France* was revised.[41]

2.11 *Last years*

In November 1955 Peter divorced Odette. A year later, in Nice, he married the former model Irene Mary Jane Hoyle. In this period, he settled in Le Rouret near Antibes, overlooking the coast he knew so well from his wartime days, and worked as a real estate agent selling local property to British clients. Here, he continued his writing, publishing a novel based on the *Maquis* des *Glières*, *By Moonlight* (1958), and a guidebook for fellow British tourists visiting the Cote d›Azur, *All About the French Riviera* (1960). We do not have much information about the character and personality of Peter, also because he had no children and the relationship with his only remaining sibling Oliver was very cold,[42] and he only visited

---

41 *SOE in France* first appeared in 1966 as an official British government publication, at a time when documentation on World War II clandestine operations was hard to come by. Michael Foot, who was a well-qualified academician (University of Manchester) and had had war experience with SAS (Special Airborne Service), agreed to undertake the task of explaining what SOE was and what it did. Although hampered by incredible restrictions from officialdom, he nevertheless had exclusive access to SOE archives. Publication of *SOE in France* represented a first acceptance by a major government that under special circumstances (in this case French concerns), the thirty-year closure rule regarding sensitive archives was not sacrosanct. However, thanks also to the libel suit launched by Peter Churchill against the author of SOE in France, the book was soon re-published with amendments in its second edition in 1968. This happened because Churchill was convinced that some parts described inside the book defamed him in some way, taking offence at something that Foot wrote about him and his role in SOE in France. So, some changes in wording were made and a new edition of the book appeared in 1968.

42 Simon Churchill, son of Oliver and nephew of Peter, told me that his father and Peter were not particularly close. There was some resentment about Peter's publication of his SOE activities so soon after the war, when it was still considered a secret organisation. Simon's mother, who worked in Bletchley Park helping to break the famous German Enigma code, had signed the Official Secrets Act and would not talk at all about what she did

the UK infrequently after he had moved to the south of France. What we know about him is found inside his wonderful and absorbing books, from his own voice, but, rummaging deeply through his personal SOE files we are able to understand something about him very interesting and intimate:

Peter has a lot of common sense. Still cheerful and humourous.[43]

Peter remained in his beloved French Riviera until he prematurely died of cancer on 1st May 1972, at the age of 63.[44]

---

during the war, even after some of her colleagues published books about their work. Peter and his brother Oliver would presumably also have had similar restrictions put on them, and not everybody was happy about Peter disclosing what he had done during the war. There is also the question as to whether Peter was exaggerating and glorifying what he and Odette had done, for self-publicity and to raise money for them both after the war. Moreover, Simon, who only met his uncle Peter twice when he was very young, told me that Peter should have been an extrovert and someone who enjoyed his life.

43   Report about Peter Churchill training in July 1941. *The National Archives*, Kew (UK) - Ref. HS 9/314 - HS 9/315 (Personal Files Peter Morland Churchill), 1939-1946.

44   Simon Churchill told me that his father did not go to see Peter in the south of France before he died, but he attended to his funeral. James Churchill (younger son of Walter Churchill born on 1937), told me that he, his brother John and their mother Joyce went to see Peter and Odette and her three daughters around 1948/49 together with the author Jerrald Tickell who, at that time, was in the process of writing a biography on Odette. The group were greeted by members of the Maquis, for whom it was a reunion for Peter and his wife. Joyce and her children went again at some point later, and went a third time in 1972 when Peter was dying. Until January 2022, nobody knew where Peter's legacy, documents and archive were, so was for his royalties but, since that date, I was able to contact Sophie Parker, daughter of Françoise Sansom and granddaughter of Odette who, before Peter, (in Boulogne-sur-Mer on 27th October 1931) had married an Englishman called Roy Patrick Sansom (1911-1957) and then moved Britain. With him, she had three daughters: Françoise Edith, born 1932 in Boulogne (died in 2018); Lili M., born 1934 in Fulham; and Marianne O., born 1936 in Fulham. Mr. Sansom joined the army at the beginning of the Second World War and Odette and the children moved to Somerset for their safety. Only afterwards Odette joined the SOE. Thanks to this contact I was able to find Peter's Eulogy, read during his funeral in Le Rouret (F). It is unknown who wrote or read it. It's interesting to learn that Vera Atkins (a senior intelligence officer who worked in the France Section of the SOE from 1941 to 1945) was present at Peter's funeral:

*"Dear Mrs Churchill, Ladies, Gentleman, Dear Friends, Dear Comrades,
If England mourns one of its best sons, France and the French Resistance
have just lost a reliable friend, a comrade of combat, and a hero of the fights
of the night of the Hitlerian occupation.*

*The French resistants, hold to the heart, the memory of the terrible years from
1940 to 1944.*

*It is during that time, difficult for our country, that Peter Churchill came to
fight on the side of those, who would not lose hope of victory for freedom and
democracy against Nazism and Fascism.*

*Member of a family of English patriots, Peter Churchill joined the French
patriots in 1942.*

*His brother, Walter, gallant participant of the unforgettable Battle of Britain
in the summer of 1940, in the R.A.F. ranks, should perish in the sky of Cyprus
during an air combat.*

*His other brother, Oliver, finished the War as Officer of the Italian partisans.
The French and Italian resistants will never forget the help received from
valiant England. Help well shown by the Churchill family, from which the
three bothers fought on French and Italian soils, and in the sky of the
Mediterranean.*

*Peter Churchill suffered the fate of many resistants. He was arrested, tortured
and deported. He was part of the 28, 000 survivors returning from the death
camps, of the 258, 000 sent to this land of distress.*

*Literature, press, cinema, television have reported the achievements of
Captain Peter Churchill. He entered history alive. He was the holder of one of
the highest English distinctions, the D.S.O. (Distinguished Services Order),
equally of the French War Cross 1939/45, he was deported resistant and
pensioner of the French war. He was Member of the Committee of Honour of
our Association.*

*In 1955, Peter fulfilled an old dream: to live on this Côte d'Azur where he
secretly landed in 1942.*

*Settled in ROURET, he was very quickly embraced by the community of this
friendly town. He reconnects with his comrades from the resistance. He joins
out Departmental Association of Deportees and Internal Resistants and
Patriots.*

*Estate agent, he contributed to the settlement of a number of Britons in our
region.*

*Of exceptional tactfulness, a lot of lively humour, very helpful, of a great
sensitivity, open to all, loyal to his friendships, of a rare modesty, Peter
Churchill knew how to win all the hearts and soon became a figure of the Côte
d'Azur.*

*So, when illness overwhelmed him, assistance was not lacking to his dear wife
Jane.*

*And so, it was these depressing months, this stubborn fight against the
relentless illness.*

*Peter was equal to himself until the end. Stoic and coherent faced with death,
as he was when faced with danger in the past, always with this touch of
humour, even a smile on my last visit the day before he died. We are proud to
have known such a man, and to have been his friend.*

Mrs Churchill charges me with the task of very deeply thanking everybody who really helped her throughout these very demanding six months for her. With Mrs Churchill, we will express all our gratitude for Mrs Stubbs, the Manager of Sunny Bank Hospital in Cannes, for her exceptional kindness and to her very devoted staff who did everything to ease these last few months of our dear Peter.

To our dear comrade of resistance and deportation, to the one who will always stay for us 'Odette', Peter's companion-in-arms, we express our appreciation for all that she did for Peter and for Jane, with her husband Mr. Hallowes.

Dear Mrs Churchill, we were the witnesses of your magnificent dedication, and also of your painful ordeal. Let us tell you of our affectionate admiration, and, assure you of our respectful and brotherly support.

I am the interpreter for every member of A.D.I.R.P., of all the deportees and imprisoned, of all the resistants and A.C. of A.M. to tell you that we share your overwhelming pain.

To Odette's three children, here present we present our most sincere condolences. Lots of very fond memories remind them of Peter.

Thank you to Miss. Vera Atkins, deputy to Colonel Buckmaster, Head of Network for Peter, of her presence amongst us for this final tribute.

Our English friends must know, that the resistants and French A.C. don't forget. Today, through Peter Churchill, they reveal their gratitude to the country that was the beacon of freedom and of hope throughout these dark years.

Farewell Captain Peter Churchill. You will always live in our hearts.

Mrs Jane Churchill asks me to offer her deepest thanks for your presence this day beside her. Please excuse her, but there will not be any shaking of hands".

PART THREE

PETER CHURCHILL'S WAR WRITINGS

The four books written by Peter Churchill after the war are extremely interesting from many points of view. First of all, they are a clear, genuine and historic mirror of the everyday life of a British secret agent during the WWII. So, before their literary importance as novels, they are important documents to be preserved as collective memory, documents which describe true facts and about one of the most terrible and frightening moments for Europe and for the whole world in the last century.[1] Moreover, his books are a sort of personal diary where he recollects all his memoir in an extraordinary confluence of details. It is impossible to think of him writing his books, even if only a few years after his war experiences, without having kept previously something like a diary or a collection of notes which could help him in this huge work. Surely, his companion and later wife Odette contributed in helping him and his memory too. The most impressive feature of Peter Churchill's works, indeed, is the massive presence of details, the incredible precision of dialogues between the protagonists of the stories, and also the vivid memory of his personal feelings during the war time.

Before summarizing and analysing Churchill's works, in this chapter I want to consider the principal literary genres concerning war writing, surely suitable with Churchill's works. I will focus

---

1   Actually only the first three books depict his personal war experience as an SOE agent, *Of Their Own Choice*, Hodder and Stoughton, London, 1952, *Duel of Wits,* Hodder and Stoughton, London, 1953, *The Spirit in the Cage,* Hodder and Stoughton, London, 1954. *By Moonlight*, Robert Hale Limited, London, 1958, is a fictional book about the Maquis des Glières who were the first French resistance group to fight a pitched battle against the Germans in World War II, who Churchill worked with during his wartime activities in the French section of the Special Operations Executive.

my research mainly to Great Britain's literature, but I will also take advantage of some appropriate examples of world literature, explaining how these literary genres appeared and evolved. Moreover, not only literary genres concerning war but also memoirs, autobiographic and historic writings, non-fiction, spy novels and other genres will be faced, to understand how they influenced Churchill's writing. Only in the end, in the last section of my work, when I will consider the main features of Churchill's writing, I will be able to relate his works to these literary genres, where they can be included and better comprehended, clarifying how and why these works have an important literary and historic relevance.

The period considered for my research will be the first half of the 20th Century, particularly texts published after the First World War experience, and those concerning the Second World War, until the end of the 1950s.

THE FIRST AND THE SECOND POSTWAR

A Historical Overview of the Genre

In the 20th Century, the two World Wars were the main events which contributed to the rise of new kinds of poetic and literary genres. These new genres arose thanks to and during these conflicts, but developed mainly in the following periods, describing the authors' war experiences. Of course, war writing was not an invention of the past century, but rather an ancient and historically consolidated genre that continues to be of vital importance even nowadays.[1] Being global, the First and the Second World Wars involved a huge number of people, fighting soldiers or civilians too, whose lives were dramatically conditioned by these tremendous experiences and by their tragic consequences. This implied the fact that also many writers, or future writers, took part or were involved in these wars and, consequently, were emotionally inspired by it in their later works. As a matter of fact, times of deprivation or crisis always pushed literature to its limits, requiring writers, to exploit their expressive resources to the maximum, in response to extremely bad events.

For decades, Britain's cultural memory of the First World War has been dominated by poetry, the principal interpretation of the war taught in schools throughout the country.[2] This poetry is often autobiographic and complements the memoirs that many writers penned in trying to express their experiences of the conflict,

---

1   The war novel's origins can be found, for example, in the epic poetry of the classical and medieval periods, *The Iliad* of Homer, *The Aeneid* of Virgil or medieval sagas like the Old English Beowulf or the Arthurian literature.

2   This is partly true also in Italy, mainly with the poetries of Giuseppe Ungaretti, Clemente Rebora, Eugenio Montale, Gabriele D'Annunzio, Umberto Saba, Carlo Emilio Gadda, Camillo Sbarbaro, Filippo Tommaso Marinetti, Guido Gozzano, Dino Campana among the others.

showing a complex and fluid relationship between autobiography and narrative. Together with poetry, it was the memoirs that figured most prominently in discussions of British writing about the war.[3] When considered together, it becomes apparent how both often take the form of an autobiographical narrative, surely because the nature of the war itself demanded a more direct response, a testimonial response. Before the First World War, at the turn of the century, a literary modernism had emerged and flourished[4] but, even if the conflict was perceived as the advent of modernity,[5] British art and literature just after the war became predominantly realistic and nostalgic. The result was that what was largely marginalized in British cultural memory was the novel.[6] So, artists were pulled back to a testimonial narrative mode, far from being modernist, and writers such as Robert Grave or Vera Brittain commented that they attempted to write fiction about the war, but ended up having to rewrite it as memoir.[7] Brittain explains it in her *Testament of Youth (1933)*:

> *My original idea was that of a long novel, and I started to plan it. To my dismay it turned out a hopeless failure.*[8]

Robert Graves, too, in his *Good-Bye to All That*, describes how he began writing his account of his first few months in France in fictional form:

---

3   e.g. Siegfried Sassoon's *Memoirs of an Infantry Officer*, Vera Brittain's *Testament of Youth*, Robert Grave's *Good-Bye to All That*.

4   Literary modernism was characterized by a break with traditional styles of poetry and verse, and experimentation with literary forms that could express the sensibilities of a modern world. Some of the key characteristics of modernist works of literature were introspection, technical self-awareness, the disruption of forms, and the development of multiple perspectives.

5   The First World War was the first modern war, where new fighting techniques were adopted, e.g. aviation, tanks and chemical weapons.

6   Perhaps it was felt that subjecting the tragic experience of the war to the imaginative process of fiction, for example, would be inappropriate, contrived, or even impertinent.

7   Saunders Max (2014) "Life Writing, Fiction and Modernism in British Narratives of the First World War", The RUSI Journal, p. 106-111.

8   Brittain Vera, *Testament of Youth: An Autobiographical Study of the Years 1900-1925*, London, Virago, 1983, p. 11.

Having stupidly written it as a novel (...) I had to re-translate it into history.[9]

It may be, then, that even critics and readers, and not only authors, felt that fiction could not do justice to the horror and scale of such a cataclysm as the First World War, and that the authenticity of history was incompatible with the novelistic form. However, the genres of autobiography and fiction cannot be kept diagrammatically apart: there are many British novels of the war that are truly autobiographical.[10] In fact, rarely writers could gain authentic knowledge of the war except through their own experiences and, in the case of Britain, the fighting was not on British soil but across the Channel and in faraway places. Moreover, the propaganda was working hard to conceal the terrible reality of the battlefields from soldiers' families, trying to hide the real face of war to the population. This noteworthy discrepancy between direct experience and second-hand, knowledge must have been obvious when the first war books came out after the Armistice until the early 1920s, when their dramatic and real stories would have seemed so revelatory. So, reading them as novels was very difficult, if not impossible at all, and the reader turned out to be the one who did the work of interpreting and translating them back into autobiographies. After the first world conflict, then, British cultural memory of it began to be dominated by the autobiographical narrative, whether in poetry or memoirs, but novels about the conflict received significantly less attention. This brings into sharp relief the central issue of how to construe the relationship between autobiography and fiction in the literature of war, which is not just a question of autobiography as opposed to fiction, but of autobiography in fiction, and fiction in autobiography.[11]

In the mid-1920s, war books, and so novels and memoirs, faced a decline in popularity and there was a feeling amongst publishers that

---

9   Graves Robert, *Good-Bye to All That*, Harmondsworth, Penguin, 1960, p. 79.
10   R.H. Mottram's *Spanish Farm Trilogy* (1924-1926), Richard Aldington's *Death of a Hero* (1929), Frederic Manning's *The Middle Parts of Fortune* (1929).
11   Saunders, "Life Writing...", p. 106-111.

the genre had passed its prime. The decline was significant and this was partly due to the pace of postwar recovery within the industry as the economy still proved sluggish. Wartime shortages carried over into the postwar period, and books were more expensive to produce after the war than before. Furthermore, the war-book market became saturated and that meant fewer book contracts for veterans with stories to tell, and sell. This reduction of titles does not signify that the public stopped buying war books, only that fewer were contracted and published. There were plenty of war books that sold well during the first 1920s, the so-called "years of silence".[12] Certainly, war books, in their many forms, had not disappeared in the 1920s and their revival appeared during the period 1928-31, the so called "war book boom" period, which saw the publication of some of the best war memoirs and novels of the age by Siegfried Sassoon, Richard Aldington, Frederic Manning, Edmond Blunden and Robert Graves. These authors, together with other foreign ones,[13] built up a sort of golden age for World War I literature. It was just a matter of demand and supply: the public was again interested in war books and publishers became speedily aware of this. The revival of war literature in general began in the late 1920s and continued into the early 1930s[14] and, after its peak in 1930, the genre began losing ground once again,[15] with readers showing more interest in novels about earlier wars.[16] In addition to this new interest, what would have contributed to the lack of interest about war writing in the 1930s was surely the war-book controversy begun in 1930. Essentially, what happened was that formal attacks on war

---

12   In January 1922, *The Blocking of Zeebrugge*, a historical account by Alfred Carpenter, and *The Escaping Club*, a war memoir by a former prisoner of war, A.J. Evans, were both listed as bestsellers.

13   Ernest Hemingway and Erich Remarque amongst the others.

14   Lawrence T.E.'s *Revolt in the Desert* was a bestseller in 1927 and the success of Erich Remarque's *All Quiet on the Western Front* created a boom out of a British revival of war books.

15   Isherwood Ian Andrew, *Remembering the Great War. Writing and publishing the experiences of World War I*, I.B. Tauris, 28 Feb. 2017, Chapter I.

16   An example could be the novel of the American writer Margaret Mitchell, *Gone with the Wind*, first published in 1936, set in the United States of America during the American Civil war.

books were made by some writers[17] who claimed that the literature of World War I presented a picture of war which was fundamentally false, even when it was superficially true, and which was statically false even when it was incidentally true. Douglas Jerrold, in his *The Lie About the War*, declared that in the war books "every essential fact is falsified" and in his Foreword he listed and examined 16 titles, seven of which are by British writers, and the others North American (four), German (three), French and Russian.[18] Most of them are novels, but there is also an autobiography, short stories and one memoir. He provided no evidence from these works to substantiate his claims of falsification, instead positing a distinction between the collective or the 'statistical', which he equated with 'history' and 'truth', and the individual or the 'incidental', which he equated with distortion and falsehood.[19] What was significant about the controversy was the association, never made explicitly, between why Great Britain fought the war and how British soldiers conducted themselves during the war. The main charge was that no war books, and therefore no writers, who presumably fought or lived the war, showed the real faces of the war, even the more dishonourable. The controversy can be summed up as a contraposition between the true historic war writing and the individual experiences which never produced unitary British narrative of the First World War.[20] All writing, whether it be novel, memoir or history, involves a process of selection, exclusion, ordering and emphasis, and intrusive, even

---

17   Jerrold Douglas, *The Lie About the War*, published by Faber, "Criterion Miscellany" series, London, 1930.

18   The titles are: Hemingway, *A Farewell to Arms*; Remarque, *All Quiet on the Western Front*; Aldington, *Death of a Hero*; Graves, Good-bye to All That; Barbusse, *Le Feu*; Babel, *Red Cavalry*; Montague, *Rough Justice*; Wharton, *Squad*; Zweig, *The Case of Sergeant Grischa*; Cummings, *The Enormous Room*; Blake, *The Path of Glory*; Herbert, *The Secret Battle*; Mottram, *The Spanish Farm Trilogy*; Thompson, *These Men Thy Friends*; Grider, *War Birds*.

19   Beecham Rodney Gerald, "Fiction and memoir of Britain's Great War: disillusioned or disparate?", European Review of History: Revue européenne d'histoire, 2015, p. 791-813.

20   The question about falsification of war writing will be lifted up again in the next chapters with the literary production of Peter Churchill, which will be subjected to some charges from others secret agents and writers.

bullying narrators can be found in instances of each.[21] So, these were some of the reasons why writing about the war, during the mid and the late 1930s, was not popular anymore, but the most important and the untold one was the fact that a new global war was perceived and felt almost everywhere, and talking or writing about the war was something people preferred to avoid.

The rash of novels that comes out soon after a war is a 20th Century phenomenon and this was true also for the period following the Second World War, which gave rise to a new development in contemporary war novels. If with the First World War the genre was dominated by European authors, with the Second World War, war novels were mainly written by American writers. The most famous are, amongst the others, Ernst Hemingway's *For Whom the Bell Tolls*, James Jones's *From Here to Eternity* and Herman Wouk's *The Caine Mutiny*, which are considered global masterpieces of the genre. For what concerns war novels by British authors, we can quote few names such as Arthur Evelyn St. John Waugh, who wrote the famous trilogy *Sword of Honour*,[22] which have obvious echoes in Waugh's wartime career, Graham Greene with his *The End of The Affair* (1951), set mainly during the flying bomb raids on London in 1944, and the Anglo –Irish novelist Elizabeth Bowen with her *The Heat of the day* (1948). However, what will be investigated deeply from here on are not only novels and literary works concerning the two world conflicts in their essence, but some of the subgenres which emerged in this new and prolific period for literature, characterized by a new description of reality. Moreover, in the next chapter, we will see how these literary frames could have influenced Peter Churchill's writing.

---

21   Ibid, pp. 791-813.
22   *Men at Arms* (1952), *Officers and Gentlemen* (1955) and *Unconditional Surrender* (1961), published as *The End of the Battle* in the US.

FICTION DEPICTING REALITY
OR REALITY DEPICTED IN FICTION?

All the literary genres I will discuss in the next sections are characterized by the same feature: the use, or the depiction, of reality. In the Tenth Book of Plato's *Republic* we can find one of the earliest discussions of the nature of imitation or representation, in which Socrates bans poets from his ideal state. He argues that imitative art is essentially deceptive, as it imitates only the appearance of an appearance, and thus is at three removes from reality, which is the ideal form. Aristotle did not agree, arguing in turn that the poet is in a closer relation to truth than the random and ephemeral appearances of nature. We can thus say that a play, a poem or a novel has never captured timeless, transcendental truth, and that the interpretations writers impose upon the natural world are merely a shadowy construct of their own minds, reflecting no natural order but only the essential formlessness of reality. The fact that the "true" reality is impossible to grasp could have created the peculiar form of the novel itself, with its ceaseless grasping after both the particular and the universal, the individual and the type, the humble and the sublime, the temporal and the timeless. Indeed, the novel has long been hailed as a form with a particularly intimate relationship to the world of daily fact, of external and temporal events, in a word: of reality.[1]

The imitation of reality has always existed in literature since literature was born, and many theorists have discussed the relationship between reality and literature. In this section, I will

---

1   Drabble Margaret, *Spy fiction*, from *The Concise Oxford Companion to English Literature*, Stringer, Jenny, Hahn, Daniel (eds.), Oxford University Press, Oxford, 2007, pp. 1-14.

concentrate my analysis on how reality can be perceived by authors and readers, especially in the literary Realism of the last century.

Realism in the arts is normally defined as something that "represents reality", the attempt to show a subject truthfully, without artificiality and avoiding any artistic conventions such as improbable, exotic and supernatural elements. What literary Realism wanted to do since it was born around the mid-19th Century was to reproduce objective reality, focusing on showing everyday activities and life. It has always tended to favour the representation of middle- and lower-class society, without any romantic idealization or dramatization, trying to depict unpleasantness, because characters with humble origins or living in poor conditions were and still are considered "more real", and common, than wealthy characters. This could be considered an attempt to symbolize reality in literature, as if it was a sort of metaphor of real happenings. Reality, or truth, is in fact the principal referent of literary Realism and, on the surface, it would appear to operate by rules set by the "real world", grounded in physical and social reality, and, consequently, outside of fiction. An objective reality, reached by literary realists, is usually depicted in the third person without embellishments or interpretations, following the belief that such reality is ontologically independent of any person's conceptual schemes, linguistic practices and beliefs. In this way, reality can be faithfully represented by writers who discover it through their senses; truth is out there and we can simply try to catch it.

Having said that, what we expect as readers is that a realist text represents its subjects as if they were "real life", and this is a common perception that the aim and privilege of literary Realism is to faithfully represent or mirror reality. Anyway, even if authors, past and present, have claimed to produce such a process in their works, they actually do not. Realists cannot be like scientists or mathematicians who reveal order and pattern through a closer and closer inspection of matter and number, and then, beyond that order, reveal a new chaos, or a new formlessness. Realist writers travel through fact to symbol, and back to fact again, in a perpetual interaction between the particular and the universal, the copy and the archetype.[2] Their literature should not be considered only an important source of knowledge about the real world, but also as able to provide another kind of "knowledge", the author's knowledge, which is richer and more varied than that afforded by empirical sciences. So, it would be a mistake of us readers to expect a direct correlation or make a direct comparison between the reality represented in a literary realist text and the external reality. Actually, modern literary Realism does not refer directly to reality, as that would be an act of imitation, and imitation is neither representation nor art, and a mere copy is certainly not art at all. Instead, literary Realism, thanks to the conventions and references the author is using, succeeds in connecting the writer with the reader in a new interaction. Differently from the theory exposed above, the status of reality, truth, meaning, and identity is not identical and true everywhere and for everyone, rather it depends on conventions that determine what kind of rules are individually or socially accepted for the con-sensual confirmation of reality, truth, meaning, and identity. Whether a statement in a certain situation and in the framework of a certain type of discourse will be experienced as real or fictitious does not primarily depend on the linguistic processes of producing and receiving this statement, but on the conventionalized decision whether this statement will be considered acceptable or unacceptable within the framework of the discourse type and in relation to the speaker/hearer's ortho-world-model.[3] There is no one reality equal for everybody, but many different world-culture realities, and they are always constructions, ontological evaluation regulated by "reality-degree-index assignment conventions" that, in our society differ from one social action system to another. In this way, we have concepts, or models of reality, in which contingencies and complexities are reduced

---

2   Ibid.
3   Schmidt S. J. and Hauptmeier H., "The Fiction Is That Reality Exists: A Constructivist Model of Reality, Fiction, and Literature", Poetics Today, Vol. 5, No. 2, *The Construction of Reality in Fiction* (1984), p. 253-274.

to meaningful structure.[4] We have our personal idea of reality, an accepted reality we can reasonably agree on, with all the parameters whereby it operates, partly informed by experience, but also by conceptual influence, including from literature. Realist authors depicts their reality and give us something to think about. Their literature has arguably helped shape our idea of reality, which has led some to claim that everything is fiction, that the scope of accepted reality, the criteria by which we define it, are indeed dictated by fiction. So, because it aims to represent reality, literary Realism implies norms and standards that may affect a continuation and naturalization of detrimental fictions.

This last argument can also be reversed, claiming that actually everything is not fiction, but reality. Normally, the term "fiction" is considered as an antonym of the term "reality" but this is a basic and misleading assumption which can be a good source of confusion when one seeks to define "reality" in literature.[5] All fiction is a means of telling us something about reality and, under this point of view, reality can be both its material and its outcome. The interaction with a text amounts to a "real" experience and has the potential of making the reader react to his own "reality", so that this same reality may then be reshaped.[6] In other words, all fiction draws on and addresses reality, regardless of genre, and, in providing an experience in itself, has the potential of changing our perception of reality. Thus, literary realism does not directly refer to or represent reality, but rather a perception of it, which it seeks to structure and communicate, and, like all fiction, draws on elements of reality, with the potential to either confirm us in our perception of it or alter it.

Some deconstructionist theorists say that, although literature might appear to provide knowledge about the real world, its reliance on language stands in its way. Paul de Man writes that:

---

4   Iser Wolfgang, *The Act of Reading: A Theory of Aesthetic Response*, The John Hopkins University Press, London, 1971.

5   Ibid.

6   Ibid.

Literature is fiction not because it somehow refuses to acknowledge "reality," but because it is not a priori certain that language functions according to principles which are those, or which are like those, of the phenomenal world. It is therefore not a priori certain that literature is a reliable source of information about anything but its own language.[7]

7   De Man Paul, "The Resistance to Theory", *Theory and History of Literature*, Volume 33, University of Minnesota Press, Minneapolis, London, 1986, p. 11.

GENRES

6.1 *Non-fiction Novel, New Journalism and Faction*

The first important distinction we have to undertake and subsequently explain is the difference between a fiction and a non-fiction novel.

A fiction novel is a relatively long work of narrative fiction, usually in prose, which describes intimate human experiences. Normally, what we can find in a fiction novel is fictionality, which is its main feature and which is most commonly cited as distinguishing novels from historiography. For the most part of the readers, when they are facing a fiction novel, they usually expect it as something not real, invented, a never happened story. Anyway, during the centuries, the genre has mixed in several ways. Especially in the early modern literature, from the 16th Century until the end of the 18th Century, authors of historical narratives often included inventions rooted in traditional beliefs, in order to dress up a passage of their books or add plausibility to their opinion. This happened also for historians who sometimes invented and composed speeches between historical personalities which surely have never been recorded, but they did it to enrich their stories and certainly for didactic purposes too. In addition, reality and fiction can mix up into a novel when this last is trying to depict the social, political and personal realities of a given place and period, trying to describe it with clarity and details surely not found in historic works.

In 1965, a series of articles made clear the frustrations with the fiction novel as a vehicle for expressing the nature of contemporary reality. Philip Roth famously depicted the mid-century American fiction writer as having:

[...] his hands full in trying to understand, and then describe, and then make credible implausible actualities that were continually outdoing our talents.[1]

So, what emerged in the mid-sixties in the USA was a new conception of the fiction novel, a new literary genre called: non-fiction novel. Truman Capote claims to have coined the term and have created this new literary genre with his 'true account' *In Cold Blood* (1966). In the same period, and always in the United States, a twin genre arose, the so-called New Journalism, which was characterized by a subjective perspective, a literary style reminiscent of long-form non-fiction and emphasizing "truth" over "facts", and intensive reportage in which reporters immersed themselves in the stories as they reported and wrote them. However, the origin and the novelty of the non-fiction novel and New Journalism have been disputed by some critics who have pointed out various predecessors. Tom Wolfe, who in 1965 published his first essay collection considered one of the milestones of the theory of this genre,[2] traces many of the characteristics of the non-fiction novel back to the travel literature of the late eighteenth and early nineteenth centuries and to Boswell's reporting on Samuel Johnson in particular. Daniel Defoe's *A Journal of the Plague Year* (1722) was noted frequently as a prototype of the genre. Contributing greatly to the debate over the novel in the 1960s was the growth of new communications technologies that provided so many disparate views of reality that no single competing interpretive frame could be deemed capable of containing them all.

Non-fiction novels are narratives characterized by the depiction of actual contemporary events and real historical figures using the styles and techniques of fictional discourse, being woven together with fictitious conversations and using the storytelling techniques of fiction. Usually, a non-fiction novel is a story the author witnessed

1   Olster Stacey, "New Journalism and the Nonfiction Novel", *The Cambridge Companion to American Fiction After 1945*, Duvall John N. (Ed.), New York, 2012, p. 44-55.
2   Wolfe Tom, *The Kandy-Kolored Tangerine-Flake Streamline Baby*, Farrar, Straus and Giroux, New York, 1965.

and/or investigated, presented in dialogues and dramatic scenes, rather than in historical summaries. It shows the point of view of the people involved, rather than from an objective distant point of view as in the classical novel, providing an immersive context in which the narration of actual events is as lively as the presentation of fictional worlds. A non-fiction novel is not fiction of course, but it cannot be considered a historical novel either, as it focuses on contemporary themes and introduces fictive story elements and, since journalistic validity is part of the author-reader contract, authors of this kind of novels frequently legitimize their knowledge through paratexts or metanarrative commentaries. Addressing subjects such as celebrities, subcultures, political protest, and court cases of violent crimes, this literature of fact tends to eliminate the distinction between élite art forms and popular culture.[3] Non-fiction novels do not follow the scientific method of history, but rather the instincts of the novelist who, usually, wants to present a true-life story as if it were a novel. This idea is extremely well explained by another important theorist of the non-fiction novel, the American critic Norman Mailer who, with the subtitle of his work *Armies of the Night* (1968), indicates the motivation behind this new genre: *The Novel as History, History as Novel.* Just as the novel mimics the cavalcade of rationally organized events that become known as history, so too is history understood as a narrative shaped by humans. Mailer goes on asserting:

> *The novel must replace history at precisely that point where experience is sufficiently emotional, spiritual, psychical, moral, existential, or supernatural to expose the fact that the historian in pursuing the experience would be obliged to quit the clearly demarcated limits of historic inquiry".*[4]

---

3   Zipfel Frank, "Non-Fiction Novel", from *Routledge Encyclopedia of Narrative Theory,* London: Routledge, 2010.
4   Klinkowitz Jerome, "New Journalism and the nonfiction novel", from *Encyclopedia of the Novel,* Schellinger, Paul (ed.); Hudson, Christopher; Rijsberman, Marijke (asst. eds.), Chicago; London: Fitzroy Dearborn Publishers, 1998, 2 vols.

Another way to call this kind of literature characterised by its non-fictional intention is the slang term: "faction", a portmanteau of the words "fact" and "fiction".

6.2 *Historical Fiction, Historical Novel, Fictional History*

The genre of historical fiction is continually expanding, adapting to new demands from readers and the creativity of the authors. Sir Walter Scott[5] is credited as the inventor of historical fiction and novel its modern form and he influenced the writing of history, historical fiction and the European and American novel for a century at least. The theory says that to be deemed historical, a fiction must have been written at least fifty years after the events described, or by someone who was not alive at the time of those events. We will also consider the following subgenres to be historical fiction for our purposes: alternate histories (e.g. Robert Harris's *Fatherland*), pseudo-histories (e.g. Umberto Eco's *Island of the Day Before*), time-slip novels (e.g. Barbara Erskine's *Lady of Hay*), historical fantasies (e.g. Bernard Cornwell's *King Arthur Trilogy*) and multiple-time novels (e.g. Michael Cunningham's *The Hours*).[6] In this sense, historical fiction itself comprises several sub-genres, and their nomenclatures are quite arbitrary. The Historical Novel Society[7] elaborated an acceptable definition of the historical novel:

Historical fiction is simply "fiction set in the past".[8]

---

5   Sir Walter Scott (15 August 1771 - 21 September 1832) was a Scottish historical novelist, poet, playwright and historian. Many of his works remain classics of both English-language literature and of Scottish literature.

6   Rodwell Grant, *Defining the Historical Novel*, in *Whose History? - Engaging History Students through Historical Fiction*, University of Adelaide Press, 2013.

7   The Historical Novel Society (HNS) is a nonprofit international literary society devoted to promotion of and advocacy for the genre of historical fiction. Founded in 1997 in the United Kingdom by bookseller, editor, and historical novel enthusiast Richard Lee, the HNS's foundational membership included such authors as Joanna Trollope, Melvyn Bragg, and Bernard Cornwell.

8   Ibid.

Obviously, this is a genre of some controversy and contradiction and this short and too simple definition brings up a number of questions. First of all, the fact that a fiction must be set in the past to be considered historical can be seen as a contradiction, considering the fact that a novel could be historical even when it is wholly or partly about public events and social conditions, which are of course material of history, regardless of the time at which it is written. Not less important, the main problem is raised by the very designation "Historical Fiction", which appears to embody a mere contradiction in terms, something that has always been a literary form at war with itself, an oxymoron (historical fiction is neither historical nor fictional). The very term, implying a fiction somehow grounded in facts, is a lie with obscure obligations to the truth, and this is suggestive of the contradictions of the genre.[9] Of course historical fiction can be many other things, it could depict real historical figures in the context of the challenges they faced, real historical figures in imagined situations, fictional characters in documented historical situations, fictional characters in fictional situations but in the context of a real historical period, or even real characters acting in a true historical period but described in a fictional way. The examples could be more, think about a historical character transported to the present, or to a time period not his own, but the most important element for historical fiction are the elements of history playing a central role in it, be they persons, events, or settings. Possessing these "elements of history" does not mean being history in the strict sense. After all, is history a right science? Is history a perfect science with no mistake? To understand if history is scientific, we could ask, for example, four soldiers about the same battle an hour afterwards. What would emerge from their answers would surely be four different recounts of the fight. Think about this kind of question after fifty or more years from the battle. Said that, it is here that the difference between historian and historical fiction writers emerges with all his impetus, historian write within their discipline, while historical novelists are not so bound, everyone of them wants to come as close to the truth as possible, but the

---

9   Ibid.

difference between their research lies in the level at which they seek the truth, the focus of their seeking. Historians focus on the events, while fiction writers focus on persons, on the characters involved in those events, that's because history is a discipline of enquiry, while historical novels are acts of creativity.[10] We can say that historians, or writers of non-fiction history, seek simply to answer to the questions "what happened?" and "why it happened that way", while writers of historical fiction are interested in explore the question "what was it like?" So, in answering the last question, historical fiction authors make full use of historical facts as they remember them and as they choose to remember them. That is why historical fiction is not about facts or events, but it is about characters and feelings, it is descriptive rather than analytical. Historical Fiction is written and read not to learn about what happened or about history so much as to live it, and it represents the closest way we can get to experience the past without being there. Reading historical fiction is a sublime personal experience: we finish a history and think "So that's what happened!" We finish a work of historical fiction, catch our breath, and think "So that's what it was like!"[11] The idea is not to report an event, but to novelize it, seeing it from within, from the limited and contingent perspective of those who are caught up in the action. To do all this requires a personal engagement, or a projection of yourself into past lives, forgetting, or pretending to forget what you know. The novelist deals with the particular, not with the general, un-like history which on the other hand is more often concerned with humanity in the plural rather than in the singular, with events and changes affecting entire societies, rather than those affecting the lives of individual beings. Instead, what matters in the historical novel is the poetic awakening of the people.[12]

Historians and historical fiction writers can help each other, the former using literary techniques for bringing history to life and the latter using historical materials to give their novels the gravitas their subjects deserve. That is why, I think, history writing requires a fictive

---

10   Ibid.
11   Ibid.
12   Wake Paul, "Except in the case of historical fact: history and the historical
      novel", *Rethinking History*, 2016, p. 80-96.

or imaginary representation of the past and, on the other hand, the writing of historical fiction can be a valuable adjunct to the work of historians in their discipline. In this way "new historians" could use narrative making their findings accessible to an intelligent public, surely larger than their usual expert reading public. Indeed, there is no reason why a historical novel may not have a research basis as good or better than that of a scholarly history and, if responsibly done, it can be an effective instrument of popular education, or at least a means for stimulating interest in the study of history. The difference between historiography and novelizing about history is of course a difference of genre, but that difference is not trivial.[13] We can say that the distinction and advantage the fictional form have is the way it uses evidence and represents conclusions. Historical fiction has the big purpose to bring history to life, and takes all those things that *were* (history) and turn something that *was not* (an imagined story) into something that *could have been* but, the truth this novel seeks is poetic rather than historiographical: it sacrifices fidelity to non-essential facts in order to create in the reader the vivid sense of what it may have been like to live among such facts.[14]

In conclusion, it can be stated that it is impossible to give to historical fiction an absolute and categorical definition, clearly each one would be contestable, not being it a scientific subject.

6.3 *Autobiographies and Memoirs*

In the corpus of World War II literature, perhaps the most urgent and significant response to the war came in the form of autobiography. From the moment that the "next war" became inevitable through the end of the 1940s, mid-term or mid-life autobiography was, for writers who expected to be killed or who felt their life had been rent in two, the most suitable genre in which to describe their experience

---

13   Slotkin Richard (2005), *Fiction for the Purposes of History, Rethinking History*, p. 221-236.
14   Ibid.

and reconcile themselves to their present circumstances.[15] Writing memoirs and autobiographical experiences, even if less than during the war, remained an urgency also during the postwar period and it surely played a relevant role in British literature of that time. The genre fitted, once again, to an urgent necessity to document personal war experiences, an intense need to leave something for posterity, a message in a bottle or a funerary urn containing the ashes of what happened to the authors of this works during that tragic moment of the last century.

Many officers, non-corporals and simple soldiers too, wrote and published a huge number of works concerning their own experiences, providing us with many different points of view about the war. One of the most famous memoirs books containing notable reminiscences about the war is *The Memoirs of Field-Marshal the Viscount Montgomery of Alamein*, published in 1958 and written by the Field-Marshal Bernard Law Montgomery, the most illustrious British officer of the Second World War.[16] The genre was prolific between 1945 and 1960, and many other important works were published during those years.[17]

Certainly, writers of autobiography and memoirs implicitly sign a pact with the reader to tell the truth, or at least the truth as they know it, about themselves. That is, primarily a subjective truth. As for facts, the expectation is presumably that this kind of writers will convey the facts as they know or remember them, but without a necessary obligation to check their memory through documentary or other research. There is no autobiographer's commitment to objectivity, rather the contrary. The autobiographical truth is, by definition, a subjective one.[18] In fact, autobiographers or author of memoirs' books are not historians, surely they were and are part of

---

15   Bolton Jonathan. "Mid-Term Autobiography and the Second World War", *Journal of Modern Literature*, vol. 30, no. 1, 2006, p. 155-172.
16   Montgomery Bernard Law, *The Memoirs of Field-Marshal the Viscount Montgomery of Alamein*, Collins, London, 1958.
17   Some of them are: W. Stanley Moss, *I'll met by Moonlight* (1950) and *A War of Shadows* (1952).
18   Fitzpatrick Sheila, "Writing History/Writing about Yourself: What's the Difference?" *Clio's Lives: Biographies and Autobiographies of Historians*, Doug Munro and John G. Reid, ANU Press, Australia, 2017, pp. 17-38.

history, they were part of historic moments, but what they tried to depict inside their works was "their history", their version of what happened during their lives and, in our case, during a historical moment as the war is. At this point we must consider all the problems and issues which can arise in such a kind of writing, and what we have to do is to show where the border between historic and autobiographic works runs.

A historian is like scientific experimenters, he does not let anything contaminate his experimental data and he try to collect documents, clues, proofs to reach and write the most objective text even written. Of course, full objectivity is not realisable, neither by historians, but it is a goal to which one need to get as close as possible and the personal or the partisan are biases and distortions that would prevent you getting at "truth". Historians don't have an explicit pact with the reader, their only task is to get the story right, implying an obligation of factual accuracy based on careful research in archives and other primary sources, which are referenced in such a way as to allow others to check their accuracy. There are cultural historians too, who are partial exceptions, since they may be after somewhat different goals, such as recovering forgotten "voices", or analysing how historical events have been remembered and mythologised, represented in different contexts and by different groups. Here, the pact of accuracy, must be accuracy of reproduction and representation, these kinds of historians, who focus on memory, are perhaps the least faithful to the positivist goal of "getting it right", since a certain relativism about the actual past is built in to the exploration of ways people remember it.[19]

On the other hand, whoever wants to write about his memories and, personal past, makes a double pact to tell the truth about himself and his own life experiences, one with the reader and one with himself, and the only access he has to respect is his own memory. In fact, autobiographic works and memoirs books are not historic works, they are literature, under all points of view, and they must be accepted as true, confirming the initial pact that everything is written is what really happened, that this is the author's "truth".

---

19   Ibid.

An autobiographer or a memoirist, in distinction to a historian, is pledged to tell the emotional truth than the strictly factual one, a subjective rather than an objective truth. As a matter of fact, one of the most important differences between historic and memoir works is the emotional part, where a memoirist is interested in arising emotions in his reader, a historian is not. This does not implicate the fact that an author who is writing his own memoir does not base himself on historical research, but this is different from an author whose writing is just the medium for presenting historical findings. It make sense to see historians as practicing a craft, using particular kind of raw materials (archives and their documents) and governed, like all crafts by various conventions about their preparation and use, a scientific writing, while writing autobiographies and memoirs can be seen as an art, in which author's storytelling is shaped by aesthetic considerations, and it can scarcely be regarded as a distinct craft or science.[20] An example of this literature can be Primo Levi's masterpiece *Se questo è un uomo* (*Survival in Auschwitz*) which significance lies less in any new "truthful" information he gives about the camp than in the artistry (with the use of literary, poetic and rhetorical devices) he employs in order to conjure up a compelling image of a cosmos utterly horrifying and at the same time present as a possibility for everyone of our time. In this way Levi ménages to demonstrate to his readers the difference between a merely truthful account of an event, of the kind provided by most survivor-witnesses, and an artistic treatment of a real event in his past which transcends the truth, reality distinction.[21]

In conclusion, historians and their works left a void that biographers and also writers of fictional history quickly filled, and professional historians have to welcome them as valuable contributors. This could be a new ensemble, and thanks to such privately revealing sources as memoirs, autobiographies, diaries, and letters, a historian could be considered as scrupulous, not touching only facts but also psychological motives.

---

20   Ibid.
21   White Hayden, "Introduction: Historical Fiction, Fictional History, and Historical Reality, Rethinking History", 2005, p. 147-157.

6.4 *War Novel and War Fiction*

War novel and war fiction, as I wrote previously, are not something new in literature, their origins can be traced in the epic poetry of the classical Greece period, especially in Homer's *The Iliad* and Virgil's *The Aeneid*, and of the medieval period, with sagas like the Old English *Beowulf*, and the Arthurian literature. This genre evolved through the years and conditioned other writings through the centuries, giving us many milestones which characterized this kind of literature, e.g. Shakespeare's *Henry V*, or the more recent Stendhal's *The Charterhouse of Parma* and Leo Tolstoy's *War and Peace*. Telling war stories, your own or those of others, has always been an act of testimony, a public ritual of healing, and it is through the act of telling these stories that their protagonists are remembered and honoured.

What will be examined in this paragraph is the rash of novels that comes out soon after the Second World War, the reasons why this happened and the mode of writing of this kind of novels. An intriguing question is why novelists write war novels or war fictions. Obviously, this counts for every war in history and maybe, on the simplest level, it is the sheer urge to record, as truthfully as possible, an excruciating, indelible, visceral experience in which the author has been physically and/or emotionally involved.[22] By tackling the subject, the author is able to come to terms with it and purge himself of the experience. As a matter of facts, unlike most other genres, the war novel needs to familiarize readers with experiences foreign to them, trying to inform the uninitiated reader about the way "it really was". Understandably, the war stories that tend to be recorded, and therefore remembered, are the stories of soldiers, the ones who carried both the guns and the wounded. So, the war novel is usually written by men, who had first-hand experience of war and it is normally intended as a mirror of the author's experiences. This strong documentary impulse usually takes the form of descriptions that provide the most

---

22   Ogunyemi Chikwenye Okonjo. "The Poetics of the War Novel", *Comparative Literature Studies*, vol. 20, no. 2, 1983, p. 203-216.

photographically accurate representations of the war zone.[23] The opinion of many soldiers or participants to wars in fact is that official histories never accurately depict "what really happened" or "what was like for them". So, the writers of this genre try to set the record straight by letting the facts speak for themselves. Although not all war novelists subscribe to a simple reflection theory of language, most narrative techniques are primarily intended to create a strong illusion of reality.[24] What this works mainly do is a mere description of facts and this, for the modern critical theory, has generally been considered of marginal importance, because it falls outside the larger articulations of narrative structure. For a long time, description was either disregarded altogether or treated as a non-functional textual luxury.[25] In fact description is different from narration, because it is primarily retrospective and contingent. The opposition between description and narration appeared already in Plato and Aristotle, where *diegesis* was distinguished from *mimesis* on the basis of direct (dramatic) or indirect (descriptive) representation. However, the technique of description is perfect for the war novel because it is admirably suited to satisfy the need both to inform an audience and to authenticate the war account. In addition, the war novel often uses description in an attempt to conceal the gap separating sign and referent and, generically, it favors description because it is less interested in the creation of characters or in the development of the plot, than in the depiction of real characters, the living conditions, the daily routines, the weapons and the equipment, the battles and the chronicles of the front. Nonetheless, this kind of works do serve another function. Creativity becomes a matter of reordering reality into patterns meaningful and psychologically comforting to both the writer and his audience, especially if the author is telling the truth. In this manner the novel serves as a confession and as a trial which makes a new beginning possible, the protagonists of the novel, the characters, may be the aggressors or the victims, are exposed and

---

23   Cobley Evelyn, "Description in Realist Discourse: The War Novel" *Style*, vol.
      20, no. 3, 1986, pp. 395-410.
24   Ibid.
25   Ibid.

then judged. So, another direct consequence of this kind of writing is that war novelists highlight moral concerns.

One of the main topics of the genre is the absurdity of war and the spirit of such absurdity is captured in many novels. One example could be the words of Ernst Hemingway in his *A Farewell to Arms*:

> *I was always embarrassed by the words, sacred, glorious, and sacrifice and the expression in vain [...] and I had seen nothing sacred, and the things that were glorious had no glory and the sacrifices were like the stockyard at Chicago if nothing was done to the meat except bury it.*[26]

In these lines it is clear the concept that the war novel of the twentieth Century tried to emphasize the anti-hero rather than the hero, broadening the perspectives of the genres with different themes, techniques, and forms. Hemingway's passage is a romantic new conception and justification for a possible soldier's desertion. Rhetorical terms like "glory" and "sacrifice" are something to go beyond and a soldier is no more obliged to follow them. If the country for which he is fighting for is in utter confusion and the armies on both sides are indistinguishable in ideology and performance, then the individual, soldier or civilian too, is entitled to dissociate himself from the society or army in order to ensure his sanity and individualism.[27]

War novel is also characterized by its attack on the reader's sensibility. Presenting the horror of war is one way of doing it, ensuring a change in the minds of the reader. Sometimes horrors are shown in all their details, trying to stimulate the reader's conscience, or trying to make him feel the pain suffered by the author. In this way, the reader can identify himself with the writer developing an act of sympathy and empathy with him, who is very conscious of the power of transmitting the horror of the war in his works.

Another really important feature of the war novel is the fact that, as reported before, it is written primarily by men, and probably

---

26   Hemingway Ernst, *A Farewell to Arms,* Charles Scribner's Sons, New York, 1929, p. 184-185.
27   Okonjo, "The Poetics of the War Novel", cit.

for men to influence them. Women characters tend to be few and stereotypically drawn. Hemingway classified women into war novels broadly into three groups: the marginally treated woman destined to be raped; the better favored female meant to be taken to bed but not married, and the advantage-seeking woman, hardened by circumstances of war and lacking any sense of honour. Of course, there are a few other groups and categories of women described on war novels, but more or less and exceptions aside, for the period we are considering Hemingway got the point.

So, war novel and war fiction can be seen and examined under many points of view, considering the fact that they are full of subjects, themes and topics that surely deserve to be analysed. Moreover, war novelists produced their works in diverse and different forms, which shed light on disparate ways of conceiving the genre: the picaresque, melodrama, thriller, satire, tragedy, tragic-comedy, historical-fiction, and mythical novel.

6.5 *Spy Novel and Spy Fiction*

The Spy novel is one of the most popular forms of fiction over the last hundred years, especially in Britain. The first form of it emerged during the international tensions of the years preceding the First World War. Scandals like the Dreyfus Affair in France[28] highlighted the activities of spies and the intelligence services that employed them, while armaments rivalries, such as the Anglo-German naval race, increased the sense of threat to national security. A new sense of national vulnerability, possible invasion, and hostile espionage let this new genre grow and flourish. It is here that the roots of the spy stories are to be found, stories in which secret agents heroes battled against the evil machinations of vile spies. The invasion scares, for example, had given rise to a whole genre of fiction depicting some imaginary invasion of Britain. The pattern of an ordinary citizen becoming embroiled in fantastic, convoluted invasion plots is played

---

28   The Dreyfus Affair was a political scandal that divided the Third French Republic from 1894 until its resolution in 1906.

out again and again in Edwardian spy fiction. One of the earliest and most famous authors of this subgenre is Sir George Chesney with his *The Battle of Dorking: Reminiscences of a Volunteer* (1871), which established the model of the genre in the last quarter of the nineteenth Century.[29] The world we can find in these novels is a dangerous and treacherous one in which Britain is considered to be the main target of the hostility, envy and even hate of the other European powers. If fear of the French, the ancient enemy, subsided slowly, resentment and hatred of the Germans developed rapidly after 1896, and Germany was more and more frequently added to the list of potential enemies.[30] From then on, Germanophobia was a central feature of the British spy novel of that time. Another powerful leitmotif in spy literature of the Edwardian age which helped to increase the genre was the national strength, or rather the lack of it. Vision of internal disorder, decline, and decadence abundantly populated the imaginative world of the Edwardian spy novel, as they did of a wide spectrum of English literature in that period.[31]

Robert Erskine Childers's *The Riddle of the Sands* (1903), a suspenseful tale of two amateur British agents foiling a German invasion plot, is often described as the first spy novel, and has become a classic. But the first spy writer to spring to public fame was William Tufnell Le Queux, whose highly successful *The Great War in England in 1897* (1894) heralded a cascade of best-sellers over the following three decades, all of which employ a series of heroic male agents cut from sturdy patriotic cloth who save the nation from the plots of foreign spies. Setting an enduring trend in spy fiction, Le Queux, who fantasized about being a spy himself, deliberately blurred the line between fact and fiction, to make spurious claims of

---

29 Stafford David A. T., *Spies and Gentlemen: The Birth of the British Spy Novel, 1893-1914*, Indiana University Press, Victorian Studies, Vol. 24, Nr. 4 (Summer, 1981), pp. 489-509.
Other examples of works depicting the spectre of a German invasion plan of Britain are William Tufnell Le Queux's *England's Peril* (1899) and Edward Phillips Oppenheim's *The Great Secret* (a.k.a. *The secret*) (1907). For the invasion novel genre see I. F. Clarke, *Voices Prophesying War, 1763-1984* (London: Oxford University Press, 1966).

30 Ibid.

31 Ibid.

authenticity and realism, and his fiction was often thinly disguised propaganda for strengthened national security.[32] As a matter of facts, Britain needed an adequate and competitive secret service, and this was a primary message of all Edwardian spy novels which brought to the revised Official Secret Act of 1911, a product of fear about German spies.[33]

Le Queux's great Edwardian rival was Edward Phillips Oppenheim, who produced more than 100 novels; amongst the best known are *The Kingdom of the Blind* (1916) and *The Great Impersonation* (1920). During the '20s and the '30s, some spy novel's writers were themselves secret agents working previously for the wartime British intelligence and painted a far less romanticized and more realistic picture of the secret agent's life, amongst them we can mention William Somerset Maugham and Compton Mackenzie. Thanks also to the works of these two writers, Eric Ambler continued their attitude crafting plots of considerable technical skill and authenticity. His best-known and most successful novel of this period was *The Mask of Dimitrios* (1939).

Graham Greene, who wrote several works before and during the Second World War, such as *Stamboul Train* (1932), *The Confidential Agent* (1939), and *The Ministry of Fear* (1943), presaged his even better-known spy novels after the conflict, during which he worked as a British intelligence officer for the Secret Intelligence Service (MI6): *The Quiet American* (1955), *Our Man in Havana* (1959), and *The Human Factor* (1978). If we have a glance at the popular novel of the mid-1950s in Britain, we can see that the theme of espionage played an important role into the narratives of war and captivity, revealing generic intersection between the spy novel, the war novel, the crime novel, and even the trauma novel or trauma fiction, concerning the memoirs of the prisoners of war.[34]

---

32   Drabble, *Spy fiction,* cit.
33   Attridge John, "Two Types of Secret Agency: Conrad, Causation, and Popular Spy Fiction", University of Texas Press, *Texas Studies in Literature and language*, Vol. 55, Nr. 2 (Summer 2013), pp. 125-158.
34   Partsch Cornelius, "The case of Richard Sorge: Secret Operations in the German past in 1950s Spy Fiction", University of Wisconsin Press, Monatshefte, Vol. 97, Nr. 4 (Winter, 2005), p. 628-653.

However, the dominating figure of the immediate post-war years for the spy novel was Ian Fleming, whose *Casino Royale* (1953) introduced the iconic figure of James Bond, surely the most fictional secret agent of all time. The Bond adventures were updated versions of Le Queux and John Buchan designed for the Cold War consumer boom, enriched with sex intrigues and some more violence episodes. By the year of Fleming's premature death, his eleven Bond spy novels, including such classics as *From Russia with Love* (1957) and *Goldfinger* (1959), had sold over 40 million copies and his hero was beginning to appear in blockbuster movies that continue to this day.[35]

The 20th Century certainly was the century of spies even though we can say that the profession of secret intelligence can be considered the world's second oldest profession. Spy fiction grew thanks to these fascinating figures but it has no definite borders and has always been a hybrid form, sliding over into many different subgenres, such as the detective, mystery, crime, or thriller, creating a clear continuum amongst them. It is stated that nearly every fourth book published in the United States and nearly every third book read in Great Britain arises from spy fiction. Just cast your eyes over the racks at any airport or at any paperback newsstand to realize just how extensive this body of literature is.[36] What makes this body of literature interesting is again its connection to reality which enables us to raise a sort of identification into the subjects. But what is most important in the study of history is what people believe to be true, far more important than the good, grey historian may later prove the truth to have been, since the historian's preoccupation is with understanding human motivation.[37] In this way, what could be true for the spy fiction works written in the first two decades of the last century could not be true for those written during the '50s or the '60s. So, the body of this kind of literature reflects reality at the broadest

---

35   Drabble, *Spy fiction,* cit.
36   Winks Robin W. and McGrew Eifrig Gail, "Spy Fiction - Spy Reality: From Conrad to Le Carre", Soundings: An Interdisciplinary Journal, Vol. 76, Nr. 2/3, Papers from the Drew Symposium (Summer/Fall 1993), Penn State University Press, p. 221-244.
37   Ibid.

level, because its trends reflect the preoccupations of different kind societies trough the times and they are a clear reflection on reality. Usually, spy fiction depicts as close as possible the realities of intelligence activity, but not always, and of course there are elements that are romanticized, that depart from reality, and that we do call it fiction. But, to be at all convincing as fiction, it is essential that it be accurate in all particulars in which it can be accurate.[38] Moreover, everyone of these particulars is of equal importance to the plot, because every simple fact inside it counts equally until one arrives at the conclusion. When reading a spy fiction, or call it "mystery fiction" too, one does not begin by prejudging which facts are more important than others, rather, at least initially, every fact must count equally, just to reach the end having considered all the possible conclusions of the tale. Reading forward, obviously some facts will be seen to be less important than others, but at the outset one must round up the usual suspects and suspect them all equally. This fiction can be considered a "democratic fiction", every fact in it counts equally, and therefore it is essential to suspend the judgment when reading this kind of novels, to be always ready for everything, just like in real life.

At this point we have to consider the figure of the spy described in such works, trying to find the main differences between spies in reality and spies in fiction. The spy in fiction is a master of disguise, delighting in grease paint, wigs and whiskers. The real-life spy is very different. It is essential to forget ninety per cent of all the spy yarns ever published, and a hundred per cent of the Hollywood films.[39] The dangerous spy is not a bit like Dick Barton or James Bond. Fleming's books are the first spy fiction utterly to romanticize the activity, that is, to become totally fiction. Bond does not do what people in real life in intelligence do, he does not gather up or analyze information, he gambles, beds, and travels. If you want to understand how a real-life spy is, picture instead a very ordinary man sitting behind a newspaper in a corner of a railway carriage, a so anonymous individual that no one would look at him twice. This,

38   Ibid.
39   Newman Bernard, "Spies in fact and fiction", Journal of the Royal Society of Arts, Vol. 103, No. 4943 (21st January, 1955), p. 131-133.

apparently, could seem an inoffensive and certainly not dangerous person, but the features described above are the true reason why he really is dangerous. He is not seeking for sensation or drama: his main task is to get information. A Hollywoodian character, with all his features, would not have lasted for ten minutes in real life, being obviously too eye-catching and noisy. This may sound disappointing, but there is worse to come. Nowadays the beautiful woman spy is an accepted character of the literature of espionage, founded also in many famous movies. In reality, the percentage of women spies respect to men was and is very low but, on the other hand, women were and are spies' first-class messengers. This is of huge importance for the intelligence purpose, for in war time the spy's biggest difficulty is not to get his information, but to get it home and this is where women are in their element, being them first class inventors of devices for evading the censor or a frontier guard.[40] In the First World War, one German woman agent used a bar of chocolate, excavating a small hole for her message and covering it again with chocolate. She was successful for a long time, until one day she dropped the bar of chocolate and broke it, revealing the piece of paper. (The bar may still be seen in the Imperial War Museum).[41] Nevertheless, spy fiction and reality have a close relationship and the spy, being he real or fictional, is very similar to the historian who gathers information making every possible effort not to contaminate its values in the act of gathering. They both are information gatherers who finally tries to verify their information, attempting to ascertain which of these may be useful. Spy fiction and spy novel can be considered as tedious as historic works in showing the real work of research and analysis, but the difference is that, if the latter don't do it, the former romanticizes this work, showing serendipity as a method of discovery, to provide us drama. However, the work itself will remain the same and spy fiction must be as real as possible, giving at least some reasonable portion of spy reality. This can be done returning to writers like William Somerset Maugham and Compton Mackenzie, real secret agents in life, who

---

40   Ibid.
41   Ibid.

showed us how intelligence really works, with fiction and romance too but only as sauce on the top of the main spy meal.

Spy fiction has always fascinated its readers with its mysteries and intriguing stories, resulting interesting because it gives access to processes taking place behind official history, to what Conan Doyle describes in one of his stories as:

> [...] *that secret history of a nation which is often so much more intimate and interesting than its public chronicles.*[42]

This idea of a national "secret history", invisible to the ordinary readers of "public chronicles" which promised to reveal the hidden causes of public events, was fundamental to the appeal of Edwardian spy novels but also to the rest of the century until nowadays. The spy novel's economy of sensation is heavily invested in this myth of "secret" or "underground" history, which both raises the stakes of the story to a world-historical level and titillates readers with access to the hidden counter-history of public events. Moreover, and more generally, for the reader and for authors too, spies have always been an attractive subject, and the fact that they are said to be almost everywhere, working in shadows amongst us, extremely magnetize our attention. This is one of the real reasons why authors began writing spy novels and spy fictions and why we take great pleasure in stories about these characters, wondering who they are and what they do. Even if technologies and society will change the way intelligence services works, spy stories will always be a truly fascinating read.

6.6 *Trauma Fiction*

Trauma, from the Greek "wound", can be both a physical "wound" or a psychological shock with lasting effect and it can be so great that it could forever threaten the integrity of the body. Trauma can be described as the response to an unexpected or overwhelming violent

---

42 Attridge, "Two Types of Secret Agency: Conrad, Causation, and Popular Spy Fiction", cit.

event or events that, return later in repeated flashbacks, nightmares, and other repetitive phenomena.[43] It is a sort of totalizing experience, an event that traumatized individuals rarely can leave behind.

During the course of the twentieth Century, trauma was recognized as a significant and complex problem and was systematically investigated and theorized by psychoanalysts, psychologists, psychiatrists, and neurobiologists. Recently, physiological psychologists report that traumatic memory is stored differently than ordinary memory in the brain. In "From Trauma to writing", Marian MacCurdy suggests that unlike ordinary memory, which is stored in verbal, linear ways in our brain, and therefore fully assimilated into the ongoing narrative of our lives, traumatic memory seems to be stored in the amygdale, a more "primitive" part of our brain that stores experience as image rather than language. Such experience is linguistically inaccessible, not known in any significant way by the survivor.[44] Cathy Caruth, in her *Unclaimed Experience* says that "trauma is not locatable in the simple violent and original event in an individual's past, but rather in the way its very unassimilated nature – the way it was precisely not known in the first instance – returns to haunt the survivor later on".[45] So, a traumatic experience becomes unrepresentable due to the inability of the brain, understood as the carrier of coherent cognitive schemata, to properly encode and process the event.[46] Traumatic memory, stored in images or icons, is pre-narrative and thus writers survivors of a trauma have to begin to order their experience into a narrative. This is not easy, but when it is finally carried out, what was frozen and static becomes something that can be better understood, revised, changed, and re-seen. This possibility of revision is the key part of narrative recovery and so, by

43   Mostafa Dalia Said, "Literary Representations of Trauma, Memory, and Identity in the Novels of Elias Khoury and Rabī Jābir", Brill, Journal of Arabic Literature, Vol. 40, No. 2 (2009), pp. 208-236.

44   Sinor Jennifer, "Inscribing ordinary trauma in the diary of a military child", Biography, Vol. 26, No. 3 (summer 2003), University of Hawai'i Press, pp. 405-427.

45   Caruth Cathy, *Unclaimed Experience: Trauma, Narrative, and History*, Baltimore, MD: Johns Hopkins UP, 1996.

46   Balaev Michelle, "Trends in Literary Trauma Theory", in *Mosaic: An Interdisciplinary Critical Journal*, Vol. 41, Nr. 2 (June 2008), pp.149-166.

complicating the self, by seeing themselves at the locus of multiple discourses and no longer frozen in one moment, writers are able take charge of their self-representation, and ultimately gain power over that which formerly imprisoned them.[47]

Trauma has been often associated, both in theory and fiction, with experiences of living through wars, the loss of loved ones, displacement from one's country of origin, or the resulting post-traumatic stress disorder (PTSD)[48] experienced by soldiers who have taken part in wars[49] or lived a devastating psychic blow from which they only rarely recovered. For example, much work has been done in relation to traumas associated with wars or with the Holocaust, and Trauma Studies have inherited, from Holocaust Studies, the idea of the unrepresentability and unspeakability of trauma.[50]

Narratives that record traumatic experiences and the scars caused by it have become more and more popular in contemporary Western literature. As readers, we have been accustomed to stories of trauma and "we follow, fascinated (though as many profess disgust), the vogue of violent emotion and shocking events".[51] Traumatic literature aims at bearing witness to trauma by representing it as something disturbing that has not been fully apprehended. Therefore, it adopts techniques which mirror the effect of trauma, following the assumption that the impact of trauma can only be represented by mimicking its symptoms through a self-conscious use of style.[52]

---

47   Sinor, "Inscribing ordinary trauma in the diary of a military child", cit.

48   Post-traumatic stress disorder (PTSD) is a mental disorder that can develop after a person is exposed to a traumatic event, such as sexual assault, warfare, traffic collisions, or other threats on a person's life.

49   Ibid, Dalia Said Mostafa, "Literary Representations..."

50   Jenny Edkins's study "Trauma and the Memory of Politics" (Cambridge: Cambridge University Press, 2003), investigates how the memories of such experiences as the Vietnam War and the Holocaust are politically constructed. Another important work on this matter is: Ruth Leys's, "Trauma: A Genealogy" (Chicago and London: The University of Chicago Press, 2000), where she traces the most important phases in the history of trauma theory starting with Sigmund Freud.

51   Miller N. and Tougaw J., "Introduction: Extremities", in N. Miller and J. Tougaw, eds. *Extremities*, p. 2.

52   Adami Valentina, *Trauma studies and Literature - Martin Amis's Time's Arrow as Trauma Fiction*, Peter Lang GmbH Internationaler Verlag der Wissenschaften, Frankfurt am Main, 2008, p. 7.

Particularly, in trauma fictions and in trauma novels very often it is unimaginable that such traumatic events remembered and narrated by the authors have taken place, and so, as in the surrealists' art, the boundary between dream and reality can be easily blurred.

The term "trauma novel" refers to a work of fiction that conveys profound loss or intense fear on individual or collective levels.[53] A defining feature of the trauma novel is the transformation of the self-ignited by an external, often terrifying experience, which illuminates the process of coming to terms with the dynamic of memory that inform the new perceptions of the self and world.[54] Other typical stylistic features of trauma fiction are: Intertextuality, repetition and a fragmented narrative voice, which deeply characterize this way of writing. Intertexts are used to give a documentary aspect to the novel, so that it will be perceived as more "truthful" and "authentic", suggesting the emergence of traces of the past in the present, a surfacing to consciousness of repressed memories: it is an act of memory which signals the haunting power of trauma.[55] In the same way, repetition imitates the symptoms of trauma indicating, on a formal level, the haunting return of the traumatic event and the disordering of chronology which characterize a traumatized individual's mind. Finally, a fragmented narrative voice suggests that history can be written and rewritten from different perspectives, and that trauma can only be worked-through if the traumatic experience is narrated to someone who is willing to listen.[56] In this way, the shocking force of trauma can only be conveyed through formal devices, by mimicking the structure of traumatic experiences,[57] and novelists can bring readers close to trauma thanks to these devices, which allow them to describe the events not in a linear or conventional way. Further rhetorical strategies adopted by trauma fiction writers are the first-person narrative and the interpellation of the reader, constantly raising questions, explicitly, but more often implicitly, to involve the reader and his personal feelings. Moreover,

---

53   Balaev, "Trends in Literary Trauma Theory", cit.
54   Ibid.
55   Adami Valentina, *Trauma studies,* p. 74.
56   Ibid, p.74.
57   Ibid, p.74.

the dilemma of traumatized individuals, and thus of trauma fiction, lies in the "traumatic dialectic between the eroding passage of time, which threatens the preservation of memory, and the fixing of time".[58] Trauma novels about war's experiences are usually written after the war, sometimes many years later, thus confirming that those traumatic events experienced by the writers are still haunting them, revealing that the effects of war, and so of traumas, are not over.

The reader of this kind of fiction, for his part, must be a true active agent, trying to assemble the pieces of the fragmented narrative, in order to give it the real meaning thought by the author. The author helps the reader getting closer to the traumatic event through the aesthetic recreation of it, giving him the opportunity to imagine how would have been being there, living that trauma from inside, not as a spectator but as a participant. In this way the reader becomes personally involved in the traumatic event and can empathize it, it becomes his personal trauma and it is precisely by inviting readers to think and take action that trauma fiction performs its task.[59] Therefore, the goal of trauma fiction is to move and wound its audience, to render the uniqueness and incomprehensibility of trauma without neutralizing its impact.[60] The reader of this fictions must abandon any expectation to reach a conclusion in the traditional sense, because trauma is caused by traumatic events, which are something not corresponding with normality.

6.7 *Witness and Testimony*

During the Second World War and in the early postwar years, a relatively rich production of diaries, interviews, biographies and memoirs can be observed. All these kinds of works are known as "Witness" or "Testimony" literature. All writers of this genre had the urge to record their experiences for eternal memory, a strong instinct inside them arouse and let them write. Michael Levine opens his

---

58   Rothberg M., "Between the Extreme and the Everyday", in N. Miller and J. Tougaw, eds., Extremities, p. 65.
59   Adami, *Trauma studies,* p. 75.
60   Ibid, p. 91.

The Belated Witness: Literature, Testimony and the Question of Holocaust Survival with these words:

> *We wanted to survive so as to live one day after Hitler, in order to be able to tell our story.*

Holocaust survivor Helen K., in an interview for the Yale University Fortunoff Video Archive for Holocaust Testimonies, expresses a sentiment voiced almost universally by Holocaust survivor, that the struggle for survival during the Holocaust was indebted to the prospect of being able to bear witness.[61] Most Holocaust survivors have a commitment to bear witness, because they feel that their testimony cannot be substituted or represented by someone else's: if the testimony is reported by another, it loses its function as such.[62] Thus, the witness's speech is irreplaceable:

> *Testimony [...] is not simply (as we commonly perceive it) the observing, the recording, the remembering of an event, but an utterly unique and irreplaceable topographical position with respect to an occurrence. [...] it is the uniqueness of the performance of a story which is constituted by the fact that, like an oath, it cannot be carried out by anybody else [...] The uniqueness of the narrative performance of the testimony in effect proceeds from the witness's irreplaceable performance of the act of seeing – from the uniqueness of the witness's "seeing with his/her own eyes." [...] In the legal, philosophical, and epistemological tradition of the Western world, witnessing is based on, and is formally defined by, first-hand seeing.[63]*

This concept is well explained in the words of the American literary critic Shoshana Felman, who calls it the "radically unique, non-

---

61   Derwin Susan, "Reviewed Work(s): The Belated Witness: Literature, Testimony and the Question of Holocaust Survival by Michael Levine", The Johns Hopkins University Press, *MLN*, Vol. 123, Nr. 5, Comparative Literature Issue (Dec. 2008), pp. 1191-1194.
62   Adami, *Trauma studies*, p. 31.
63   Felman S., "In an Era of Testimony: Claude Lanzmann's *Shoah*", Yale French Studies 97 (2000), pp. 105-106.

interchangeable, and solitary burden"[64] of the witness, expressing one more time the recurring question of the irreplaceability and uniqueness of being a witness.

Since the end of the Second World War, "we are living in an era of testimony"[65], and that is because such large-scale traumatic events produce millions of testimonies who want to bear witness. For survivors of such tragic events as the Holocaust or wars, writing their witnessing was and is a hard process that leads from catastrophe to creativity, a challenge with themselves, considering the complexity of being a witness. The testimonies of war's experiences or Holocaust survivors represented the emergence of a new mode of writing all the same: Elie Wiesel, in his *The Holocaust as Literary Inspiration* writes about it:

> *If the Greeks invented tragedy, the Romans the epistle, and the Renaissance the sonnet, our generation invented a new literature, that of testimony.*

Most of these survivor writers assume that literary ways of expression construct for the reader the events of their tragic experiences as a total reality, pointing up the validity of a vast human and historical truth. Moreover, the literary, inherently fictional formulation of the testimony constitutes the appropriate vehicle to transmit the image of each writer's world.

So, testimony is a form of responsible speech that addresses the other, and it offers the reader or listener the possibility of a personal connection with events in which he or she was not directly involved.[66] The survivor has the responsibility to bear witness both for all his/her friends he/she had lost and for those who were not there during the tragic time he/she witnessed. The function of a testimony of a historical or tragic event and his consequent literature is usually believed to be that of establishing the facts of the historical facts he is narrating, of proving that it happened. In this way, a "true

---

64   Felman S., "Education and Crisis, or the Vicissitudes of Teaching", in C. Caruth (ed.), *Trauma: Explorations in Memory*, p. 15.
65   Hartman G., *The Longest Shadow*, Indiana University Press, 1996, p. 104.
66   Adami, *Trauma studies*, p. 32.

testimony" is often conceived as an important key, with which we can open the door and be able to see how the original event actually took place. However, recently, post-structuralisms challenged this idea, arguing that the meaning of testimony should be relocated in the survivor's subjectivity.[67] In fact, in recent years, witnesses are consulted more and more by historians during historical documentaries but, what emerges from their witnessing, is always a version of the facts, their own version. Survivors, in most of the cases, are not historians, but simply human witnesses to a difficult situation, sometimes dehumanizing, and what is more important is the relationship originated between them and their listeners, between witnesses and their audience. Only at this level testimony becomes a vehicle of collective memory, and no more an expression of the author's individuality, it becomes a dialogue between past, present and future, and a process of reconciliation of both listener and survivor with the past.[68] In my historical essay "La Ricerca di Katarina",[69] on the subject of testimony about a specific traumatic war event, I wrote:

> *Reality is a product of the moment in which it is happening and, already there, in that precise moment, it becomes subjective, individual, property of those who are its protagonists (and witnesses), those who, living in that moment are conscious about it and have their own opinion about it. From that moment on, there will be many versions of the same reality, but no one could ever be objective and correct as that specific moment.*

---

67   Ibid.
68   Ibid, p. 33.
69   Cominini Andrea, "La Ricerca di Katarina", in *Studi e ricerche di storia contemporanea n. 83-84*, Anno 44°, Istituto Bergamasco per la storia della Resistenza e dell'età contemporanea, Bergamo, giugno-dicembre 2015, pp. 74-82. "La realtà è figlia del momento in cui essa accade e già lì, in quel preciso istante, essa stessa diventa soggettiva, parte propria di coloro che ne sono i protagonisti, di coloro che partecipandovene ne hanno coscienza e ne hanno un'opinione. Da quel momento in poi ne esisteranno molte versioni, ma nessuna potrà mai essere oggettiva e corretta come quel momento stesso".

PART FOUR

PETER CHURCHILL'S LITERARY WORK

Peter Churchill complete catalogue includes five books. The first three can be considered as a trilogy, depicting his own experience as a secret agent of the Special Operations Executive from 1941 until the end of the war in 1945, *Of Their Own Choice* (1953), *Duel of Wits* (1954), and *The Spirit in the Cage* (1955). His fourth book, *By Moonlight* (1958) is a fiction novel, but the background story of the French Resistance group called "Maquis de Glières" is true in every detail. Churchill's last book is titled *All About the French Riviera* (1960)[70] and it is merely a tourist guide about the French Riviera, written for English tourists.

In my work, and particularly in this and the following section, I will consider, describe, and summarize his first four books concerning the Second World War, works which can be easily included, for their features, in all the genres described in the previous section: non-fiction novel, historical novel and fiction, autobiographies and memoirs, war novel, spy novel, trauma fiction, witness and testimony.

The first two books, *Of Their Own Choice* and *Duel of Wits*, are written in the third person, and Peter narrates his stories under the code-name of *Michel*, even if he reveals his true identity in a short-hidden passage between the lines in the first pages of his first work:

> *[...] As he put his hands on the rails he turned his head saying, "I didn't quite catch your name." "Churchill, sir." "Right, Churchill. Let's have a look on deck." [...]*[71]

---

70   Churchill Peter, *All About the French Riviera*, Vista Books, 1960.
71   Churchill Peter, *Of Their Own Choice*, Hodder and Stoughton, London, 1952, p. 44.

However, it is only with his third book, *The Spirit in the Cage*, that the author reveals unequivocally and frankly his actual identity; developing the entire plot in first person, and using his real and complete name. This helps us to rebuild his whole war experience as a secret agent, unifying this third book with the two previous one, thus converting them into a real trilogy of his personal war service. So, I think it is necessary to provide a short synopsis of Churchill's books to better comprehend the plots, the characters, and the main features of these works, which will then be analysed in the subsequent chapter.

Figure 1. Peter Churchill on January 1950
(photo donated by Peter to his brother Oliver on 25 January 1950).

7.1 *Of their Own Choice (1952)*

Michel is one of the fourteen recruits who will attend their first course of sabotage at Wanborough Manor (UK), learning intensive instruction in this school of subversive activity. He and his companions are the first SOE (Special Operations Executive) recruits and will be trained to become secret agents and later sent on the field. After some weeks of training in different places, Michel, together with only two others, pass the course and so is sent on a kind of post-graduate course in specialized railway sabotage.

It is December 1941 and Michel get his first French cover name, *Pierre Chauvet*. At that moment he is a Lieutenant in the Intelligence Corps, well trained also as a parachutist. The headquarters assigns him his first mission in France, explaining it in every detail, adding that everyone in this kind of business is a volunteer, and every job is of his own choice. Michel, who is French-English bilingual, is very happy and excited, but also worried about the imminent mission and, during a short period of spare time, he begins thinking about his brothers, the younger a secret agent in the SOE just like him and the older a pilot in the Royal Air Force.

Michel reaches Gibraltar on a Polish ship called S.S. Batory and here his real identity is revealed for the first time, his true name is Churchill. The trip lasts seven days and here he has time to perfectly memorize all the details of his mission, before reaching his new accommodation in Gibraltar. Here he meets some Officers and agrees about all the details for the new mission to come. He is supposed to reach the French coast by submarine and so he chooses a specific coast point that he knows very well, having spent time in the region before the war. The trip from Gibraltar to the French coast inside the submarine lasts seven days and during it he learns everything about submarines, becoming friend of all the crew.

One night, at about 800 yards from the coast, Michel greets the crew and he reaches the prearranged French beach by canoe. He is frightened during his short journey because the sea is rough and big waves make the trip seriously difficult. As he reaches the shore, fear doesn't disappear, because now he is conscious to be alone in an enemy country, and everything depends on him. However, having reached this precise point makes him happy, because it reminds him the beautiful summers spent there before the war. He lights up a cigarette and begins walking to reach Cannes through hidden paths. It is winter and it is very cold but, after many kilometers under rain and snow, he reaches a safe house in the district called "La Californie", where a known caretaker lives. Here he finds a couple who helps, hides and feeds him and, after having slept, he takes a bus to reach Antibes.

In Antibes Michel meets Doctor Louis and his family, local Resistance organizers, and gives them 450.000 Francs as prearranged with the headquarters in London. In the doctor's villa he meets also Bernard (Baron d'Astier de la Vigerie) who is the Resistance chief in Lyon and who asked him to join him in his imminent trip to Lyon. Before leaving for Lyon, Michel is able to send a telegram to London headquarters where he explains that the first mission called "Operation Annabelle", consisting in providing money to the local Resistance organisation, is fully accomplished.

Michel and Bernard, after a pleasant train trip, reach Lyon and Michel is able to understand from Bernard's tales how the Lyon Resistance is operating. In Lyon Michel has to face a document check and, because it is the first time in his life with a new identity, he is very frightened about it, but everything goes well and he passes with no trouble. It is January and the weather is very cold. Together with Bernard he goes to the Resistance headquarters where he meets many local Resistance members. Later on, he reaches the Hotel de France, his future dwelling, and the following day, after some difficulties, he meets *Germaine* (Virginia Hall), an American woman working for the British Intelligence. Thanks to *Germaine*, Michel receives the important food-tickets, necessary to eat in the Vichy France, and then he meets, amongst others, a local Resistance chief called Charles. Michel gives Charles a sum of money and asked him to find suitable fields for future airplane landings, showing him all the feature that such a field should have. In addition, he promises Charles that a radio operator will be sent from London to join his organisation and to facilitate the communication with the British headquarters. Soon after, Michel takes care to sends a telegraph to London explaining that also "Operation Leonore" is accomplished.

After this new success he finds himself alone in a café for a drink and begins think about his parents and his brothers. Maybe, he wonders to himself, whether they are doing the same thing, for it is his 33rd birthday.

Michel leaves Lyon to reach Marseille on the morning express. Here *Germaine* is waiting for him and leads him to Olivier, an Englishmen working for the Resistance French Section. Thereafter he meets a certain Colonel Deprez, a manager of a large ice factory and also the leader of the local ex-Service Men's League. During this frightening meeting, Michel tries to convince the Colonel to do his best to facilitate the release of ten important men imprisoned at St. Nicolas prison using his great influence. Unfortunately, although Michel promises him a huge reward, the Colonel declines to offer his help and Michel comes back to *Germaine* and Olivier, explaining this bad news. At this explanation Olivier tells Michel that he would help him in this important mission and Michel accepts, giving him 1.000.000 Francs for the operation. Finally, he lets *Germaine* send a telegraph to London explaining that this last operation isn't fully accomplished yet.

At this point Michel has finished his job in France and tries to find a way to return to England. Now, one of Olivier's couriers has to bring him to a man called Tomas who will help him to reach Spain thanks to a little boat. When they finally find him after a long and difficult research, monsieur Tomas tells them that his correct name is Dumas, and that unfortunately he cannot do anything for Michel, because his brother's boat, used for the clandestine trips to Spain, is no more in his possession. So, Michel begins to think of another way to reach Spain and considers crossing the Pyrenees.

Meanwhile, while he is walking on the streets of Marseille, he finds his way barred by two men of the Service d'Ordre of a new branch of the Vichy Government police and is asked for his documents. Michel produces his card right away, but the men see the huge lot of banknotes in his wallet and, to let him free again, they ask him for it. Michel accepts and soon after he reaches Olivier in his apartment where he finds *Germaine*. Here they tell him that the two men weren't S.O. cops but two gangsters who robbed him of 25.000 francs, but also that actually the Germans and the fascists are arresting people all around the city to bring them to Germany as workers, just because they aren't able to find any volunteers. *Germaine* then explains Michel that travelling to Spain alone is very difficult and dangerous, and so she offers him her presence during the dangerous trip until the border, acting as if they were a real couple.

Michel and *Germaine* reach Perpignan in the south of France, very near to the neutral Spain, after a train journey. They settle in a hotel and later they find a Russian man called Popofski who, after being paid 5.000 Francs, suggests a guide to Michel. *Germaine* returns to Lyon. The following day everything is arranged and Michel and his guide are ready to depart for the long trip across the Pyrenees. Suddenly a telegram from *Germaine* arrives, asking Michel to stop the operation and go to Clermont-Ferrand for an important matter. So, Michel takes the train and reaches the place only to discover that this unexpected change of program was totally unnecessary because the matter was not as important as it seemed. On the way back to Perpignan, Michel meets *Germaine* once again and she gives him the name of a local trustworthy guide. Before leaving, Michel thanks *Germaine* and tells her that he is happy that everything went well and that the Resistance movement has received all the necessary money to continue their purposes.

Arrived in Perpignan, Michel meets Pasolé, his new guide. Together with a Spanish man called Manuelo, they take a taxi and during the trip they suddenly stop in the middle of nowhere. It is deep night and they all get out of the car and begin walking.

The trip is very hard and difficult because all the paths are narrow and it is a completely dark night. Moreover, they have to pass through some little mountain villages and, in some occasions, they are chased by the villagers who want to catch and consign them to the authorities. After two nights and seventy-five kilometers zigzagging through the mountains to reach a point far only eight kilometers, the three men reaches Pasolé's farm, where they meet his brother. Here Michel pays the service of his guide who immediately goes back to Perpignan for further guide trips.

After a lively car trip with some Pasolé friends, Michel arrives to the village of Bañolas, where he meets Pasolé's nice and welcoming family. Here he is able to send a telegram to the London headquarters explaining all his recent movements and later he reaches a luxury hotel in Barcelona. The following day, together with a Belgian Officer and the Consul-General, he reaches Madrid where he meets Captain Coburn, who was with him in Gibraltar at the beginning of his missions and who proposes him to reach Gibraltar together. Michel accepts and succeeds in crossing the Spain-Gibraltar border while hidden in the boot of the car.

In the Gibraltar headquarters he is informed that an aircraft will take him to England that same night. The aircraft has some problems with its engines and doesn't start properly but, after midnight of 14th February, it finally takes off. At dawn, after eight hours of flying, while the coasts of England are just visible, one of the aircraft's engines failed and they begin losing height. However, the pilot executes a masterly landing on Portreath aerodrome's small airstrip, even if in these precarious and difficult conditions. Once landed, Michel meets Captain de G. from headquarters, who congratulates with him for his successful mission.

Figure 2. In 1952, while he was writing his first book, together with Odette,
Peter used to give speeches about their war experiences
"Behind the Lines in Occupied France".

7.2 Duel of Wits (1953)

In the introduction the author explains his previous book and reveals, with no doubts, that he was actually a secret agent. Michel arrives to the London headquarters and everybody acclaims him. His chiefs notify him the fact that the following day he would be promoted to Captain and proposed for a decoration. Michel is bursting with joy. Soon after he is informed about his new mission, called "Mission A". According to this, Michel now has to deliver some radio operators and a complete radio set to the French Resistance movement. So, he once again reaches Gibraltar and subsequently, by submarine, the same French coast point of his last mission, where he is able to accompany the radio operators and give the radio set to his old friend Louis. Michel then leaves the coast and comes back with a canoe to the submarine together with Bernard, and then drops off to more SOE agents nearby, completing his second mission. The submarine now heads the Italian coasts. Here, they sink a huge Italian ship and succeed in stopping another one whose crew is interrogated. Afterwards the submarine engages in a battle with a German U-boat and Michel is very frightened but nobody sinks anybody. In the end the submarine comes back to Gibraltar and Michel can finally come back to England once again.

In the London headquarters, Michel is proposed for a new sabotage action. Together with the Newton brothers he would knock out a radio station near Paris called Ste. Assise, very important for the German's long rage communication with their submarines in the Atlantic. He asks his superiors for some days for thinking about it and then he goes visiting his family. Once back, and after all the explanation and every detail about the mission, Michel accepts it and knows his new companions who will work with him. Before leaving for the mission, the three men have a long period of training for the mission, studying every little part of it. On 28th May 1942, the Newton brothers and Michel are ready to be boarded on the Halifax but, right at the last second, Major de G. arrives and warns everybody that the mission is fallen through. This is caused by the fact that the headquarters was warned that a numerous German regiment is patrolling the surroundings of the Ste. Assise radio, because an independent French saboteur had been caught while trying to knock out the radio station.

May, June and July pass and only at the end of August Michel is proposed for a new mission. He has to act as a Liaison-Officer with a certain *Carte*, the French chief of a big Resistance organization in the area of Montpellier. His job will consist of providing money, setting up new launch fields for men, weapons and goods, finding appropriate fields for planes to land, and organizing new sabotage actions. His cover name will be *Pierre Chauvet*. Michel, preferring the action, is not very happy about this mere job of organizer and delegator, but finally accepts. During the night of 27th August, he is parachuted on the countryside near Montpellier.

For the first twenty-four hours Michel wanders through the fields changing his clothes and hiding the parachute. After one night he reaches Montpellier, where he takes a train for Cannes. Here he goes to his friend Antoine's villa where he is assigned his new radio-operator Julien, and later telegraphs London about his safe arrival. Having met *Carte* he is addressed to his new house in Antibes, which will be his future headquarters, and gets acquainted with Suzanne, who shows him where the radio set is hidden and who will be his future trusty partner. During these days Michel meets many exponents of the Carte's Resistance movement, but he is not satisfied with the low security in which they are operating. He is also not satisfied with his radio operator and, after having sent seven reports about the current situation to the London headquarters between 10th September and 8th October (signing it with the name of *Ramon*), he gets a new radio operator named *Arnaud*.

Arnaud is very a different type from Michel but they understand each other very well and, after some difficulties in sending and receiving messages to London, they begin a new mission with the General de Lattre de Tassigny, consisting in providing weapons, money, and food to his group of partisans. Michel now is happy because his job is bearing the fruit he expected. Meanwhile Suzanne finds a very clever method to finance the movement, reaching the sum of 15.000.000 Francs.

During this period, Michel has to find a work to justify his presence in France, otherwise he could be deported to Germany as a worker and so becomes an "estate agent". Suddenly some problems arise because 3 radio sets are broken, but *Arnaud* succeeds in repairing every one of them, also one set in Toulouse, 600 km far from their headquarters. Michel is truly satisfied about his new radio operator. On 2nd November 1942, more SOE agents arrive, four men and three women, who are immediately sent to operate in different villages and cities; amongst them there is Lise. Michel likes her very much and considers her pure dynamite. Lise has to go to operate in Auxerre, but Michel is able to keep her with him for a short period assigning her some "dirty jobs" which she fully accomplishes.

In this period Michel is very worried because he has too many situations which must be kept under control and he cannot sleep at night about it. Moreover, he has some trouble with *Carte* about the way he is conducting his job. In fact, Michel thinks that *Carte* and his organization work "too loudly" for being a secret and outlaw movement. For the moment he transfers himself to a house in Antibes and begins to organize a new action against the Italian troops which soon will occupy the area. The idea is to blow up the Frejus tunnel between Italy and France to delay the occupation. Meanwhile he receives a message from London headquarters where he is asked which sabotages he has carried out until now, but he gets angry about it because his mission is to be an organizer and not a saboteur, considering the question senseless and offensive.

Lise now has to go but Michel asks London headquarters to keep her with him. Lise bet 100.000 Francs that he would not succeed in it, but she loses. Then, a message arrives to not blow up the Frejus tunnel, as they had been planning, and let the Italian troops invade the area.

Another new mission is ready for Michel. "Mission Vinon" consists in finding an appropriate filed for a plane landing but, after many surveys, he cannot find one fitting all the features required. London headquarters asks why he hasn't found it and, after his explanation, they agreed for a new landing and Michel promise a new suitable field. Meanwhile the true identity of Michel, which of course is not the estate agent *Pierre Chauvet* but Peter Churchill the secret agent, is accidentally divulged. Feeling betrayed, Michel moves to a safer villa in Cannes, while he is informed that his old headquarters house in Antibes has been searched and that the police asked for him.

On 12th December, Lise, Michel, and other collaborators travel to Arles and settle in the Grand Hotel Nord Pinus. After some tricks performed by Lise on some German Officers they, together with a local Resistance chief called Victor, begin searching for and inspecting new fields suitable for landing, waiting for new instruction from London. Time passes by but no message arrives and they spent a few weeks in Arles waiting for news. Only after Christmas, on 27th December, they receive the long-awaited message that announces the arrival of an aircraft which will deliver new men and bring others back to England. At night they reach the prearranged field, but Michel is not able to catch and signal the airplane because they misunderstood the timetable with London. Back in Arles Michel argues with *Carte*, who tells him that he would prefer to collaborate with the Americans rather with the English.

It is during this period that Michel begins to grow fond of Lise, who he doesn't see simply as a coworker anymore. Lise seems to reciprocate feelings.

In January, *Carte* resigns, and *Paul* (Henri Frager) and *End* (André Marsac) become the new leaders of the Resistance movement, even if he continues his role unofficially. Michel is happy about the new chiefs and soon after finds a new and more suitable landing field. The airplane arrives and, though some complication with the landing operation, it takes off successfully, after having accomplished his mission.

Lise and Michel come back to Cannes for the last time and then they arrange for a new landing in the countryside of Basillac, a small village 800 km from Cannes. Once here Michel finds the field and waits for messages from London. One night, after having reached the field, they immediately begin signaling the airplane with some torches, but suddenly some German soldiers arrive and comb the area. Everyone runs away and hides and, the following day, after having seen many Gestapo members around the village, Michel and Lise decide to leave the area. After having reached Toulouse, they are informed that many of their friends have been captured, so *Paul* and *End* propose them to travel to Haute Savoie, in the French Alps, which will be surely safer for them. It is February 1943.

Arrived in the village of St. Jorioz, on the shore of Lake Annecy, Michel finds an encouraging atmosphere. Here he changes his cover name in *Pierre Chabrun* and settles himself in the Hotel de la Poste run by Jean Cottet and his young beautiful wife Simone. Together with Michel, Lise, and *Arnaud*, there are other collaborators: Jacques Langlois, Jacques Latour and Gervais. The place is perfect and the population is helpful. On the second half of March, Michel learns the fact that 2.000 men of the Maquis de Glières, a free French Resistance group settled in the surroundings, need armaments, and so he telegraphs London asking for it. The weapons and all the necessary are parachuted some days later and therefore a plane is arranged to come and pick up Michel, bringing him back to London headquarters once again.

Michel reaches Tournous and subsequently Compiègne before having passed through Paris for a short visit to his friend Charles Fol and his family. Here he is finally able to get on a plane and arrives in England. It's the 24th March and this was his seventh attempt to come back home.

Once in the London headquarters, Michel summed up all his last months in France to his superior Officers. He realizes that this time his return is very different from the previous triumphant one, now it is like nothing has passed. Soon after, Michel goes to visit his parents and sadly understand that his brother Walter, an "ace" pilot in the Royal Air Force, has been shot down and killed in action in Sicily.

After returning to London, he is informed that his friends Suzanne and *End* have been captured and that Lise has found a German secret agent called "Colonel Henri" working around. The headquarters advise her to avoid him and Michel asks to come back and definitely fight with a weapon in his hand, now that the Maquis de Glières group has been armed. He is tired and frustrated of his old job, always fighting an eternal one-sided duel of wits where one stands so little chance if he's caught unarmed. In the evening of 15th April, Michel returned to Haute Savoie by aircraft.

Waiting for Michel, Lise, Jean and Simone have to climb a high mountain in the snow to reach the point where he will be dropped. Here they light up some bonfires to signal the aircraft their right position. The group is excited and as Michel lands everybody hugs each other. Together with Michel there are also six others parachutes with weapons, clothes and food to be delivered to the local partisan

group. Then, they all go to an abandoned old Hotel where the
parachutes are burned. The return to St. Jorioz village is very hard,
difficult and dangerous. Lise falls down on some rocks and faints.
Michel is very worried, but she wakes up and he carries her on his
shoulder for the rest of the trip. Once again in the Hotel de la Poste,
Lise tells Michel that they have 36 hours before Colonel Henri, the
German secret agent, would show up and make a move. Michel
trusts her. Soon after they telegraph London that everything went
as planned but this will be the famous last words. In fact, one of
their couriers called Louis le Belge, together with the double-agent
Roger Bardet, betrays them and sends Colonel Henri to the Hotel
to catch them. The hotel is now surrounded by Italian and German
troops. The first captured is Lise and then it is Michel's turn. Colonel
Henri asks him if they prefer to be prisoners of the Italians or of the
Germans and he replied the former. Each are shut in different cells
and Lise is not able to sleep because of the mistake she has made.
From this moment on, Lise and Michel enter the long, dark parallel
tunnels of their solitary passage through the valley of the shadows,
towards death or survival.

Figures 3, 4, 5. Haute Savoie (F), municipality of Viuz-La-Chiésaz.
Commemorative plaque on the top of Semnoz, the mountain where Peter
Churchill was dropped on 15th April 1943 (Marie Baud's Archive).

7.3 *The Spirit in the Cage (1954)*

16th April 1943, Midnight. Day 225 behind the lines for Peter, and he and Odette has been just captured. Their first gaolers are Italian, who bring them to the Annecy prison. Peter cannot sleep and is very worried for Odette's fate. One day he tries to escape while a guard has entered his cell, but the only thing he is able to obtain is a confinement into a safer cell, after being beaten hard. Afterwards, Peter and Odette are boarded on a lorry and transferred to Grenoble.

They remain in Grenoble's jail for ten days and here Peter, thanks to an Odette's lie, begins to be suspected for being a relative of the British Prime Minister Winston Churchill. Soon after, they are transferred once again and, before reaching Turin and later Nice, they agreed to confess that they are married, agreeing upon all the details for the future interrogations. Driven to Toulon, the two prisoners are consigned to the Germans, escorted by car to Marseille and finally travel to Paris by train. Colonel Henri is waiting for them at the station where he drives them to their new prison of Fresnes.

Peter has the cell nr. 220, on the second floor, and begins his new life in it. The other prisoners call him from the other cells and they all know each other. Peter is given the name of Louis. Colonel Henri pays a visit to him and tells him that also his radio operator *Arnaud* has been captured. After that, he tries to convince him that he could be exchanged with the important Rudolf Hess, who was then imprisoned in England. This is thanks to the fact that they believe him a relative of Winston Churchill, but Peter doesn't trust him.

Time passes by and Peter is very sad about the situation. In his loneliness he thinks about Odette and misses her very much. Besides, he is very hungry and is waiting for his first interrogation. In the meantime, he is able to meet Odette and spend a quarter of hour with her and this fact is very helpful for his nerves. From this moment on, Peter begins the new path towards the faith and becomes very religious.

One day he, Odette, and other prisoners are brought to an elegant building in Paris where they are interrogated. The Gestapo officer tells Peter that they know everything about him and his action as a secret agent. He acts dumb but he isn't tortured, maybe because of his surname. At night, all the prisoners are brought back to Fresnes. During the following days, in the cell Peter learns how to communicate with his friends by tapping in Morse code on the wall or talking through the tube of the outside cistern, and this alleviates his imprisonment. Again, Colonel Henri comes to Peter's cell and asks him if he knows somebody who can send him extra food parcels from outside and that, in the case, he will arrange for everything. Peter doesn't trust him, but Henri gives his word of honour. So, Peter asks time and begins to think about Monsieur Fol, one of his friends living in Paris. Meanwhile, he receives the first of many visits from a Wehrmacht Priest named Paul Steinert, who helps him both spiritually and materially, giving him a German grammar and other books. The days in Fresnes are very difficult for Peter, making him swear to himself that, if he ever survives this mess, he will never complain about anything as long as he lives. Henri comes back to his cell once more and asks about the matter of the food parcels. Peter gives him the address of Monsieur Fol. After that, Monsieur Fol comes to Fresnes and, together with Peter and Henri, they agree for the food parcels to be delivered, also for Odette.

August is drawing to an end and one day Colonel Henri takes Peter away with his car apparently for interrogation. Actually, he brings Peter to the Fol's apartment in Paris and they have a rich lunch together, spending the afternoon playing piano and singing gaily. Back in Fresnes prison, Peter thinks about his past life in freedom, about his friends and his parents. At the end of September, he has his second interrogation and he continues the village idiot act as he did in the first one.

During October, many of Peter's mates in Fresnes are deported to Germany, but Father Steinert advises him that Odette is still there. In November, the guards call every prisoner to take their finger prints and photographs for the criminal records, and so Peter is able to meet and speak with Odette. Amongst other things, she tells him that, during one of her interrogations, she admitted to be the grey eminence of the South France Resistance movement, and that Peter was only a numb-skull member, unconsciously supporting his position of being dumb.

1943 finishes and on 13ᵗʰ February, after almost 300 days in Fresnes prison, Peter is advised that he will be transferred to Germany. After a journey in a private car, he reaches the Gestapo's quarter in Paris, where he is questioned by the local Gestapo's chief, who tells him that they are sending him to Berlin and finally back to England. Peter is astonished about it, but cannot believe the officer and does not trust him at all. Before leaving, he asks him if Odette will travel with him to Berlin, but the officer denies.

At midnight, Peter and two civilian German guards reach the Gestapo Headquarters in the Albrechtstrasse – Berlin. After a short interrogation he is sent to his cell, where the slow routine of prison life begins once more. During this time Peter can see many bomb raids carried out by the R.A.F. on the city. On 2ⁿᵈ March, he is not transferred to England, as he had been promised, but to the Sachsenhausen Concentration Camp, a Protective Custody Camp not far from the city of Oranienburg.

Once in his hut, Peter is welcomed by an Irish Sergeant who tells him that now he is in the Sonderlager "A", a special camp for political prisoners, sometimes called Sonderhäftling or Prominenten. In the camp Peter makes friendship with two Italian high officers, two Polish airmen, and some Russian officers. He is very happy about his new accommodation, because here he is free to go out and do many things forbidden in his previous jail. He begins thinking that probably all these important personalities shut in this camp will be used as hostages in the future. His meaningful surname could be another clue for this theory. Days pass by in the camp quietly and Peter have plenty to do, books, walks, music, bridge and, sometimes, he discusses about politics and war with his Russian officers friends. The only thing that breaks this calm are the increasing raids from the British R.A.F. and the American Air Force.

Summer arrives and new elements are introduced into the camp, amongst them there is Colonel Jack Churchill, but not a relative of Peter or Winston Churchill. He and Peter decide to pretend to be cousins and both related to the Prime Minister. All the prisoners are conscious that they are very privileged in this part of the lager, and this is confirmed also by the occasional bursts of machine-gun heard sometimes during the night and coming from the main camp, where "normal" prisoners are detained.

Some friends of Peter, who have been escaped from other camps and that now are in Sonderlager "A", organise an escape by building an underground tunnel and ask Peter if he wants to join them. He declines, explaining that for him, as a political prisoner and supposed to be a relative of Winston Churchill, it would be highly inadvisable to do so. They accept his decision and begins digging the tunnel. Meanwhile, Peter thinks about his beloved Odette, where the fate could have sent her, and hopes about her good health. During the night of 23rd September, the five tunnel men decide to escape and, once outside the camp, they divide themselves into three groups, disappearing in the night's shadows. At 7.00 a.m. of the following day the pandemonium breaks loose in the camp. As soon as the Gestapo arrive on the scene, the interrogations get under way for each prisoner. When Peter's turn arrives, and when he is asked why he didn't join his friends in their escape, he answers that he is not a prisoner of war, captured in uniform, whose escape is recognized by the Geneva Conventions and that for him is better to remain in the camp waiting for the developing of the events. After the interrogation, the Gestapo officer assures him that they will recapture his friends very soon, because they do not have a chance.

After this important event, Peter carefully observes how the camp's life is evolving and suspect that amongst the prisoner there could be a traitor who failed the tunnel's building affair. Soon after he easily discovers him. Calling him with the false name of "Judd" he is able to make him confess his dirty role in the camp and, thanks to the co-operation with the other prisoners and some tricks, succeeds in keeping him calm, also for his future safety. Peter continues his long discussion with his campmates about the war and how it could evolve, when one day he is informed by a guard that his five escaped friends would have returned to the camp very soon. So it is, and the following day they are brought back.

Peter has the chance to know each one's destiny after their epic escape for freedom in the night of 23rd September. Wings and Jimmy's escape lasted only about 24 hours, when an unknown member of Hitler Youth saw and signaled them to the police, that sent them into another lager. Jack Churchill and his mate James were able to catch some trains and then hide into the countryside for several days but, in a place not farther than twenty-five miles from the Baltic Sea, they were captured and separately sent to Gustrov Jail. Also Major Johnny Dodge, who escaped alone, caught some trains and soon reached a farm where he hid and where he was helped by two French and a Polish worker. Unfortunately, one day the German farmer discovered him and, after having warned the police and the Major was also sent back to imprisonment, one month after his escape.

Everything is ok until the second week of April, when the whole camp is quickly packed and ready to be transferred elsewhere. Driven to the station, all the prisoners catch a train and reach Flossenburg Concentration Camp. This place is shocking. The sight of the smoke rising from the crematorium chimney and the bad condition of the prisoners reduced to naked walking skeletons are nothing but terrifying for everybody. Luckily, five days later, the prisoners continue their journey and travel for 36 hours in few sardine-box vans without windows, reaching Dachau Concentration Camp, where they are housed in a hut full of other political prisoners. Here Peter discovers what it means to be a real Prominenten, because all the prisoners boxed together are important political, military or diplomatic personalities. Driven to Innsbruck Concentration Camp around 21st April, Peter is able to speak with one of his companions in misfortune, who was before in Ravensbrück prison camp and who tells him that she met Odette and that she was fine.

At the end of April, the prisoners are put on buses once more and set out for the Brenner Pass. The convoy, consisting of three coaches and escorted by some S.S. guards, reaches a village called Villabassa, in the Puster Valley in Italy. During a break, one of the prisoners finds a document, in a guard's wallet, declaring the fact that twenty-eight members of the prisoners must be executed. At this point, the Wehrmacht Colonel Bogislaw von Bonin, who is a prisoner himself, goes to the post office of Villabassa and telephones Kesselring's Fourteenth Army Headquarters in Italy, asking for a company of the Wehrmacht to come and rescue them from the hands of their murderous S.S. guards. The company is promised for six o'clock of the following evening. Now all the 132 prisoners, including Peter, housed in the local hotels, live in suspense, waiting for their destinies. That evening Peter listens to the breathtaking story of Lieutenant Fabian von Schlabrendroff, depicting how his attempt on Hitler's life failed and how consequently he was arrested. One night passed with no problems and, the following day, the S.S. guards leave, after being warned by von Bonin about the imminent arrival of the promised Wehrmacht Company. Once arrived, the prisoners are taken to the Pragser-See Hotel, situated 5.000 feet up on the mountains, a lovely place near a lake in the middle of the Italian Dolomites. Everybody now is more relaxed and calmly settle down, waiting for the arrival of an American company to take them over from the Wehrmacht. The news that Hitler has committed suicide reaches the radio set of the hotel and now the collapse of Germany is inevitable. The American troops arrive at the lake on the fifth morning, bringing with them blankets, cigarettes and food for all the ex-prisoners.

It is May and Peter now is driven to Verona, where he is boarded on a transport airplane that reaches Naples. He remains in the Allied prisoner's clearing house for some days and, after having tried with no success to bring to England with him one of his Russian friends called Stefanov, who shared most of his captivity, he is finally flown back to England in the personal aircraft of Air Marshal Garrow. England. It is 12th May 1945. Once landed, a car escorts him to the new offices of the French Section of SOE in Oxford Square – London, where he sees Odette waiting for him, still alive and in good health.

Little by little, Odette tells Peter her dreadful story, which will be accurately and sensitively told by Jerrard Tickell in his book *Odette* from which Herbert Wilcox made a film with the same title.

Later, Peter and Odette join Oliver, Peter's younger brother, returned from his long service with the Italian Section of SOE, and go to pay a visit to their eighty-year-old father, founding him in a grief-stricken state. Having lost his eldest son in August 1942, followed by the death of his wife in September 1943, as Peter had feared while he was in Fresnes prison, where he had spent nearly two years in solitude.

On 17th November 1946, Peter and Odette are amongst the 250 personalities who are awarded with George Cross by King George VI in person, during an investiture ceremony in Buckingham Palace – London. Odette is the first and only woman decorated that day.

In the appendix of the book, the author reports all the destinies of the most important figures appearing in his work, thanks to his huge work of research.

Figure 6. Odette Sansom in FANY uniform (First Aid Nursing Yeomanry – Princess Royal's Volunteer Corps), London 1946.
The National Archives, Kew (UK) – Ref. n. HS 9/648/4.

7.4 *By Moonlight (1958)*

In the initial note, the author specifies that the book is a work of fiction, but the background story of the Plateau de Glières is true in every detail, adding that all the names mentioned therein are the actual names of the men who lived this epic story of the French Resistance.

Frank Bishop is a twenty-five years old Squadron-Leader pilot who is driving his car through the Cotswolds in England while suddenly he sees a girl on the road with her car stuck. Before having warned his friend and colleague Mike in the airfield, thanks to a nearby telephone box, he gently accompanies her to London. During the trip they know each other better and he explains her that he is returning from his own Investiture by the King. From his conversation, Christine understands that Frank is the best friend of her brother Mike and she tells him that she knows many things about him. Once London is reached, they greet and promise to keep in touch.

Frank is an intelligent man who studied foreign languages in Cambridge and who already have survived the most dangerous air battles of the war with his spitfire. At the aerodrome he meets Mike and tells him about his encounter with Christine. Surprised, Mike then arranges for a threesome dinner at the Leicester Arms and this will be the forerunner of several such evenings over the following weeks. Towards the end of October, Frank takes Christine down to his workshop showing his wood sculptures and they both confess their love for each other.

In November, Mike and other pilots fly to the coast of France for a short mission, but he doesn't come back. Frank is desperate about this loss and advises Christine. The Commander then asks Frank if he wants to have a Station job as a Wingco (Wing Commander), adding information about a Resistance group of patriots in France, called Maquis de Glières, who have been equipped and supplied by the British R.A.F. He is impressed about the stories of these brave and courageous men, and finally accepts the new work proposal.

Frank goes to meet Christine's parents, where he did a good impression on them and soon after he reaches his mother's house where he stayed for the night, before his new job in Tempsford (a secret British airfield used by the Special Operations Executive). The following day he is explained about his new tasks and is introduced to his new companions. He will work with Pierre Maréchalle, an expert French navigator who already dropped eighty-seven men by parachute and a great number of containers in the most impossible places all over the France for the various Resistance movements. The commander explains Frank that, for first, he will be sent on two or three trips with Maréchalle as second pilot, so as to get the hang of things, and only subsequently he will have his own crew. Frank begins his training and makes the first flights with these heavy bombers, founding them very different from his previous light and lively fighters, dropping the first men and containers. Meanwhile Pierre tells him everything he knows about the France Resistance, especially about the Maquis de Glières and how they have been fed by previous R.A.F. missions. The young pilot is more and more attracted by his wonderful stories about these unbelievable men.

Frank now writes a letter to Christine where he asks her to marry him after the war. Christine replies and accepts, making Frank the happiest man on earth. Unfortunately, they cannot meet for Christmas because of his new job and all his training. Indeed, the first mission for Frank is now ready. He has to pilot a huge bomber over French territory and drop a load of containers on the Maquis of the Vercors. Pierre will act as his navigator.

One late evening they take off and, during the flight, Pierre explains Frank how the French Session of the War Office, through a BBC radio programme, warns the partisan with special code messages of the imminent droppings. Their message for that night's mission is: "The squirrel shakes its bushy tail". While flying over France, they are shot by flak, from German anti-aircraft artillery, but with no serious problems. As they reach the dropping zone, they can see the bonfires on the mountains set in a rectangle marking area, this is the partisan's signal. The bomber drops its entire load and they begin their trip back to England. Suddenly Dennis, the co-pilot, finds Pierre unconscious, but he can't find any wound over him, only a tiny spot below his chest, probably caused by a splinter of shrapnel of the previous German Flak attack. Pierre faints and everybody is .

now trying everything possible on him. Immediately they contact Tempsford aerodrome, warning them about the critical situation. "All South aerodromes standing for your landing" is Tempsford's reply. Pierre is in a coma and his heartbeat is constantly checked by one of the dispatchers. The way back to Tempsford is difficult because the crew doesn't know very well the best route, being Pierre the flight's navigator. Near the city of Rennes, German Flak batteries open fire at them and one of their engines is damaged. Nevertheless, they reach England, which is under a thick wall of fog. Tempsford advise them to land at Portreath aerodrome, which has special flood-lighting, and the bomber finally arrives. Pierre is quickly taken to the hospital but soon the news of his death reaches the crew.

Back in Tempsford, Frank writes a letter to Christine and later is informed about his next mission. This same night he will fly with twenty-nine others aircrafts, trying to drop important armaments to the Maquis de Glières. Frank is happy for this new mission, but sad about the fact that Pierre will not be with him. Al the details are explained and the take-off is at 7.45. During the trip, five bombers are shut down by the German Flak, but soon they reach Semnoz Mountains, where the Maquis are waiting for them. Suddenly, Frank's bomber is attacked and many bullets reach it causing a fire. The crew parachutes out the aircraft and Frank, with a difficult operation, is able to make a dangerous emergency crash-landing on the snowy mountains, not far from the partisan's bonfires.

When he opens his eyes, he can see a small group of men standing beside him, one of them is Tom Morel, the commander of the 500 partisans of the Maquis de Glières. Tom tells him to hide for some days, until they will be able to ask London an aircraft to pick him up, but Frank places himself at his command, telling him that he wants to fight with them. Tom gladly accepts and introduces all his men to the new arrival, making Frank doesn't fell like at home. The following day, Marc, one of Tom's helpers, explains Frank how and where the Maquis de Glières exactly works, revealing him its famous motto: "Vivre libre ou mourir" (To live free or to die). A message to London is sent, explaining that Frank is still alive after his crash and that he will remain with the partisans to fight the French Militia and the Germans.

A new life begins for Frank, who is able to see with his own eyes and understand all the old Pierre's tales about these brave Frenchmen patriots. He begins patrolling the area with other partisans, demonstrating and practicing with Brens, guns and Sten guns. Moreover, he can see how the Maquis is supplied with foods and goods by the valley folk. Soon, London reply message arrives, asking Frank to advise them for a new aircraft pick-up as soon as this will be possible. Moreover, they warn him about the right place of landing and specify that Goddard's partisans will be his helpers for that operation. Now he is happy, because Christine surely knows he is alive and in health and a great relief comes over him. After some days on the Plateau, Frank becomes a liaison officer attached to the various headquarters and he is given the war-name of *La Pape*, being the translation of the surname Bishop - l'Evêque to obvious.

Soon after a betrayed truce from the commander of the Militia, Tom decides for action. The plan is studied in every detail but Frank is asked to remain on the Plateau, this being a private French battle. He accepts and 100 partisans leave to face the Militia. The following day, while Frank is waiting for their return, nothing happens until the late afternoon, when he can see some figures coming back slowly in the snow. Unfortunately, he discovers that Tom and his friend Geo have been killed in action, after having captured many members of the Militia. Both the fallen have solemn funerals and are buried on the Plateau. From then on, Anjot, one of Tom's best friends, becomes the new Commander.

After the action against the Militia, an entire German Division of seasoned mountain troops with heavy artillery surrounded the Plateau. 8.000 Germans and 1.200 Vichy men begins their partisan's hunting, but the French patriots are determined to make an example out of Glières, to serve as inspiration for the rest of France to break the bonds of occupation. The first night, all the chalets and the shelters of the partisans are bombed and so the men must sleep outside or inside some makeshift igloos. The fight lasts for all the following day and night but it is too unfair and Anjot decides for the retreat. The men of the Plateau are dispersed and most of them have been killed in action but Frank is able to send a message to London, asking for a next pick-up as soon as the danger is past.

In the meantime, he has reached a chalet hidden in the mountains and takes shelter there for some weeks, thanks to the old couple who guests him. London reply arrives, warning him about a new aircraft pick-up for the next moon. At this point he tries to reach the Goddard's group of partisans but, during his journey, while on a bus, he is captured by the French Militia in Annecy. Frank is brought and locked up in a dirty cell of the Annecy Fort.

Because of his false identity card, which shows the French surname of *Tardieux*, his gaolers do not believe him being a Wing Commander of the British Royal Air Force. A Major of the Wehrmacht asks him the number and the base of his squadron but Frank denies, saying that he cannot give him this important information. Some days later, the Sturmbannführer Karl Ullricht, chief of the Haute Savoie Gestapo, comes to his cell for an interrogation, asking him the same questions of his Wehrmacht's colleague, adding the fact that if he would collaborate, he will be immediately transferred to a special prisoners' camp for captured R.A.F. officers in Germany. Frank denies one more time and Ullricht leaves, giving him time to think about his proposal. The following days trapped in the cell are very hard for Frank but, thanks to a file hidden in his clothes, he begins to cut the steel bars of his cell's window.

One day, Ullricht comes again, warning him that he knows everything about his next meeting with the aircraft and adding that he personally will receive it in style, helped by his own team of men. This thing will surely get him a decoration and a promotion. As the Gestapo officer leaves, Frank keeps working on the steel bars with his file, while he constantly thinks about his beloved Christine. Finally, one night he is able to break all the steel bars of his window's cell but, while he is escaping through it, some guards enter his cell and catch him again. Ullricht arrives and tells him that the High Command has decided to recognize his status as a R.A.F. officer and that he has orders for his transportation to Germany. On the afternoon of what is to be his rescue day by the R.A.F. Frank is led to a lorry and driven away but, after some kilometers, it suddenly stops because a tree is just crashed down in the middle of the road. It is an ambush. The local partisans rescue Frank and capture his German guards. After that, Goddard, the commander, lead him to their headquarters, explaining that they have followed his story from the beginning and that have arranged everything for his imminent pick-up. At this point, Frank tells Goddard that Ullricht and his men will reach the landing point too, trying to capture the aircraft and its whole crew. So, everything is arranged for Ullricht's squad to be arrested too.

Once arrived to the prearranged landing field on the mountains, Goddard's partisans and Frank impatiently wait for Ullricht's arrival. As the aircraft has landed, Ullricht reveals himself and reaches it, capturing the pilot with no troubles. While he is triumphantly coming back to his car previously hided not far away, Frank, Goodard and his men suddenly show them up and disarm him and his troop. Frank thanks Goodard and his partisans and soon after boards on the aircraft, bringing with him the handcuffed and no more confident Ullricht. The aircraft takes off.

Once back in England, Frank reports every part of his story to his headquarters. Soon after he meets Christine, who is extremely surprised and happy to see him back home. Frank and Christine marry, before the end of the war, and he continues his work in the army, before as a Wing-Commander and later in the Intelligence Service. After having been awarded the George Cross by the King, Frank promises his wife to bring her to Annecy and to the Plateau of Glières one day.

Eight years have passed and Frank and Christine finally have their long-promised pilgrimage to France. Now they have a son, a little boy called Michael who is happy about this holiday but is too young to understand the real purpose of their visit. The family goes to the big "La Morette" cemetery where Tom Morel and many other Frank's friends are engraved and, once on the Plateau, they find a small stone monument in honour of *La Pape*, the brave R.A.F. pilot who supplied and fought beside the Maquis de Glières in their battle for freedom.

Figure 7. Peter Churchill in the 1950s.

PART FIVE

THE MAIN CHARACTERISTICS OF PETER CHURCHILL'S WRITING

Peter Churchill's writing is very interesting under many points of view. Before examining its characteristics, we must consider some aspects related to his person and education, because I think they have been fundamental in his personal development.

Churchill, born in 1909, was a member of an upper middle-class family, which brought him around the world during his childhood and later established in Cambridge. His father was a British Consul and an art historian, his grandfather an archaeologist, and everywhere we look in his lineage, it is possible to find beauty, class and culture. Because of his father's job, Peter was born in Amsterdam and, before 1923, he lived in Sweden, Italy, and Algeria. From 1923 to 1927 he established in Geneva (Switzerland) where he was educated at Malvern School and later at Chillon Castle and Geneva University. He grew up bilingual in French and could speak Italian and Spanish fluently, and languages have always been one of his favorite interests leading him to one of the most popular, and difficult to access, university of the world, the University of Cambridge, where he read Modern Languages. All these aspects about his early years will condition his future writing, which will be very cultured, detailed and surely not predictable.

My proceeding way in analysing the four war books of this forgotten author will follow an unconventional path. In fact, instead of examining one book at a time and chronologically, I will explore Peter Churchill's emblematic characteristics of writing through his entire work. Moreover, where this is interesting, these same features will be compared to the literary genres analysed in the second chapter.

8.1 *Descriptions of characters*

> *Her name was Lise and from her mop of light-brown hair, swept*
> *back to reveal a rounded forehead, down to a pair of discerning eyes,*
> *there emanated a distinct aura of challenge that was only intensified*
> *by the determined set of her chin below a somewhat colorless face.*
> *[...] But what took and held his gave above all else were the hands;*
> *hands such as he had never seen before in his life. They were long with*
> *slim, capable fingers and, as the left one held the wineglass and the*
> *other broke off pieces of cake, he observed the telltale expanse between*
> *thumb and forefinger, denoting extravagance, generosity, impetuosity;*
> *the ambition in the index fingers; the unusually wide gap between them*
> *and the second fingers, showing independence of thought only matched*
> *by the independence of action that almost cried out from the gaping*
> *valleys that lay between the fourth and little fingers. At the moment,*
> *the second and third fingers on the left hand were overlapped in a shy*
> *gesture, as though seeking each other's company – or was it to hide the*
> *platinum wedding ring that had not escaped his eagle eye?*[1]

One of the exceptional qualities in Churchill's writing is surely
his ability in describing of the characters he encounters during his
war missions. The passage above describes the first meeting with
his war courier *Lise* (Odette), who will marry him after the war.
Undoubtedly, he is bewitched by this pleasant vision and, like a
thunderbolt, it is love at first sight. The punctilious description of her
hands is a blend of the typical aptitude of the secret agent, scratching
for any important detail, and the insistence of an enamoured look,
not believing in something ever seen before. The way he illustrates
every single finger is not only precise, but crosses the gates of poetry,
consigning us a highly poetical and romantic piece right inside a
war book. The description of *Lise* continues several pages later on
this same level, mixing poetry and sentimentalism, but adding even
something magical and mythological to her figure:

> *[...] she was always happiest among the marvels of nature and her*
> *love of trees was quite remarkable. During the moments that she retired*
> *inside her shell of solitude to commune with nature and eternity, Michel*

---

1   Churchill Peter, *Duel of Wits*, Hodder and Stoughton, London, 1953, p. 155.

felt himself cut off from her like a complete stranger. At such times it was as though she came from another world; as though she had a secret which he could never share. It was as if she had lived for centuries and was much older than he.[2] *[...] she was a most attractive girl. She may have been 30, as she said, but nobody – man or woman – [...] would have put her at a day over 23. Not that age has anything to do with charm; it was simply that she represented eternal youth.*[3]

In addition to *Lise*'s description, which is evidently conditioned by his inner feelings for her, Churchill presents us every new character with a great ability in portraying them. Every time this happens, thanks also to all the apparently insignificant physical particulars, it is as if we could see the new figures in front of our eyes. Moreover, the author has the capacity of explain in a few words the personality of each one of them, and not only their physical nature, suggesting us their future behaviors throughout the plot, and thus conditioning our judgment of them.

The boss of this group was clearly Bessonov, a short powerfully-built Georgian with black teeth, close-cropped hair, a strong determined jowl and eyes that were a mixture of devilry and merriment. Added to these features he had a soft creamy skin and on hearing on his deep voice and husky wicked laugh, one had a fair picture of the generally accepted notion of a Mongol bandit. Still, thirty-eight-years-old Jan Bessonov struck me as being an attractive character.[4]

Bartoli was six feet tall and had been through the Abyssinian campaign. By trade a pastry-cook and waiter he could make a cake out of porridge, condensed milk and cocoa. He was brave, loyal and an asset to the community; besides this he was a natural comic.[5]

A classic feature in Churchill's description is the use of figures of speech, particularly similitudes and metaphors, skillfully used to characterize his subjects and their personalities, but also to enrich

---

2   Ibid, p. 213.
3   Ibid, p. 248.
4   Churchill Peter, *The Spirit in the Cage*, Hodder and Stoughton, London, 1954, p.135.
5   Ibid, p. 143.

his writing. These features enable him to give us short but very clear and definite descriptions of the persons depicted in his works.

> *[...] I was drawn most by the outstanding personality of Colonel Ferraro of the Italian Partisans. A tall, powerfully-built man with a ruddy complexion and curly brown hair, he smoked his pipe placidly amidst the hubbub and looked for all the world like a champion golfer waiting patiently in a crowded club-house for his turn to tee off.*[6]

After these examples taken from his trilogy books regarding his war experience as a British secret agent, I think it is necessary to mention also descriptions found in his work of fiction *By Moonlight*, where he probably assumed a different attitude, not being conditioned by reality and by his photographic memory. In fact, descriptions in a work of fiction can surely be freer, following the fantasy and the poetic vein of the author:

> *He looked up as the door flew open and Michel Bennet strode in. Mike was a generous six-foot, broad shouldered, mighty of arm, a Viking, with a mane of corn-gold hair, which Frank suddenly found most fascinating.*[7]

> *As Maréchalle watched his drink being poured, Frank took stock of him. The man must have been forty-five at least. He had a thatch of thick graying hair over a dark, rugged face of a flat, wide-nostrilled nose; a moustache, the blue chin of a man who has to shave twice a day, a short neck and broad shoulders. He was very nearly six feet tall.*[8]

> *He saw a young face with intense brown eyes looking out from below thick eyebrows, a straight forehead and closely cropped hair. Small ears, one of them set a little above the other, gave the face a pixie look, but the warm mouth and the glow from the eyes quickly cancelled out that impression.*[9]

---

6   Ibid, p. 205.
7   Churchill Peter, *By Moonlight*, Robert Hale Limited, London, 1958, p. 17.
8   Ibid, p. 48.
9   Ibid, p. 93.

Churchill's depictions of his characters, both in his autobiographical and in his fictional works, demonstrate his natural talent in writing, not only providing us new names to enrich his plots, but also giving us a perfect and complete shape of the new incomers, molding them with their emblematic physical and psychological features.

8.2 Intertextuality and Trauma

Intertextuality in literature is the interconnection between similar or analogous works, or parts of it, that reflect and influence an audience's interpretation of the text. Authors use this device, which creates a correlation between texts and generates related understanding in separate works, to get to the point easily. Very often, it is easier to seek help from the words of another author to express your own feelings or particularly difficult concepts. Usually, the author is being quoted has previously expressed such ideas in a way that is perfect for new present condition and so there is nothing to add about it, just quote their words. Moreover, these kinds of references are made to influence the reader and add layers of depth to a text, based on the readers prior knowledge and understanding. Intertextuality is a full-fledged literary discourse strategy that comes in handy when authors are not able to express their feelings properly.

Churchill, surely thanks also to his academic studies, makes large use of Intertextuality in all of his novels, but the most interesting use of it is in his third book *The Spirit in the Cage*. In this novel the author describes all the events happened during his period of imprisonment, from April 1943 until May 1945. Most of these facts are traumatic and they will change his view of life forever.

I now began to think of the cigarettes, the drink, the food and all the other joys of life that I had always taken for granted. Now everything was a luxury including food. With the meager rations I supposed that one could just about keep body and soul together. I had read Victor Hugo's Count of Monte Cristo, and so already had a fair notion of what dungeon existence was like but, try as I might, I could not remember a single passage that had dealt with the gnawing pangs of chronic hunger. Perhaps man's power of evil had increased since the days of the Chateau d'If.[10]

Here, Churchill's use of Intertextuality is clearly winking to his reader, who has to be a smart literate reader, conscious of who Count of Monte Cristo is and what happened to him. The interrelationship between the author and the protagonist of the Victor Hugo's novel is obvious, both living the same difficult situation of starvation chained in a cold and dark cell. Churchill admits he has never been in such a situation, and the only way to represent himself into it is to seek help from his literary studies, which maybe would help him in finding a solution. The interconnection between a traumatic circumstance and Intertextuality, between the description of a traumatic situation and another literary work, is typical of Peter Churchill's writing, and here follows another tremendous example:

> *We drove off through the gates and headed north. Yellow signs at every cross-roads, bearing the dreaded indication of Oranienburg, soon told me what to expect. Just before the war I had read Louis Golding's Mr. Emmanuel which unfolded the doubtful pleasures in store for anyone who entered the gates of Sachsenhausen Concentration Camp. So that was it. I should now experience the terrors that Golding had so vividly described as to make the reader feel he was sharing them with the unhappy Mr. Emmanuel. I braced myself to bear the blow of what now seemed my certain fate.*[11]

Once more, the tragic situation asks for a parallel example with a literature work where the same traumatic event has been lived before. In this case Churchill quotes a very recent literature work for that time, being Louis Golding's *Mr. Emmanuel* first published in 1939, only four years before his own imprisonment. Just like Mr. Emmanuel, believed to be a spy, he is imprisoned in the same concentration camp and, thanks to Golding's work, Churchill is able to imagine the terrific experiences that are waiting for him.

Further on, the author describes one of his meals in the camp,

---

10   Churchill Peter, *The Spirit in the Cage,* p. 46.
11   Ibid, p. 125.

this time quoting a German writer:

> *[...] eating alone was not the sad affair that it had been and always must be for the man or woman in solitary confinement of whom Goethe might almost have been thinking when he wrote: "Nur wer die Sehnsucht kennt, Weiss was ich leide, Allein und abgetrennt von alle Freunde..." (Only those who know longing, knows what sorrows me, alone and separated from all joy...)*[12]

In this case his feeling is of relief. After his arrival in the camp, he understands that he has been assigned to a "lucky" section of it, being he considered a political prisoner. This means that he would have been well treated, or almost not like all the other ordinary prisoners destined to the crematorium. Once more, he makes use of literature to express feelings in traumatic moments, in this case quoting the poem *Nur wer die Sehnsucht kennt* of the inventor of the Weltliteratur, the German author Johann Wolfgang von Goethe.

As we have seen, especially in his fourth book, Churchill lived many traumatic experiences during his captivity, beginning writing his feelings in a particular way and with characteristics typical of the trauma fiction (even though it is not writing fiction) explored in the second chapter. The author, before his own imprisonment, had never been a religious person but all the traumatic events lived "in the cage" will transform him and his faith forever.

> *Turning away from this swiftly vanishing image and joining my hands in my first serious prayer, I said out loud: "Oh God, let me behave with dignity that I may deserve such honour." As I said these words I was aware that, for the first time, I have invoked God's help. Up till then I had thought I was self-sufficient.*[13]

This is the first passage where he discovers his faith and begins trusting in God as he has never done before. The captivity in solitary cell at least gave him the possibility of thinking very much, time wasn't something he was lacking. In this way he reached his personal

---

12   Ibid, p. 132.
13   Ibid, p. 49.

conclusion about the relationship between this lonesome condition
and religion, trying to understand and comment every section of
"The Our Father Prayer":

> *I concluded, that the Zen Buddhists packed off their novices into the
> Himalayas to spend several years on a snow-capped mountain peak
> simply to contemplate the sound that would be made by the clapping of
> one hand, before they were considered fit to come down and be initiated
> in the fundamentals of this sec. "... as we forgive them that trespass
> against us."*[14]

Churchill had never been captured before and, although he
had lived 225 days behind the lines before his capture, he was
accustomed to an easy life, especially thanks to his social status.
What he experienced behind the bars, starvation, cold, solitude and
even blows, were unthinkable and unbelievable for his person, and
his spirit would have been undermined surely also for his future life,
as confirmed in the last passages of this paragraph:

> *In every way but one the prisoner is slowed down to a stand-still. The
> one exception is his mind. This keeps travelling at the same rate, if not
> faster, than it did in freedom. Unhampered by interruptions and outside
> influences, it grasps more quickly and penetrates more deeply than it can
> when moving continuously from place to place at the speed of modern
> transport. It is as easy to travel for twenty minutes in the underground
> and think practically nothing as it is impossible to spend the same amount
> of time in a cell and do likewise [...] If movement is life, then stagnation
> is a kind of death that seems very real to the prisoner.*[15]

> *I now fell into the habit of cutting up my bread into so many lumps
> of equal weight and eating these every two hours or so with plenty of
> water. Thanks to my astonishing powers of sleep, my regular exercises,
> [...] my prayers, [...] I realized that the Lord was doing everything
> possible to help me pass the time with patience. [...] I swore that if ever
> I survived this mess I would never complain about anything as long as
> I lived.*[16]

---

14   Ibid, p. 51.
15   Ibid, pp. 87-88.
16   Ibid, p. 82-83.

8.3 Excellent and inspiring "Spy Writing"

Undoubtedly, the genre where Peter Churchill's writings best fit is spy fiction. Actually he was a spy, a secret agent sent by the British Intelligence to work behind the lines in a foreign country full of enemies. After having read his books, we can say with no hesitation that being a secret agent was a second skin for him, something he really liked to be. Of course, when he began writing, all this passion for his role came out under the shape of a really good "spy writing", enabling him to give us high literature pieces of this genre. Being a spy especially means having a sixth sense, the insightfulness of a bloodhound, and Churchill saved his life many times using it in the darkest moments of his career during the war. One perfect example is shown when he, after being conducted to the main Gestapo headquarters in Paris by his gaolers, is proposed to be exchanged for a German lieutenant currently in British hands. Only his shrewdness and intuition would have saved him from what he understood to be a bluff:

> *At Gestapo headquarters I was led upstairs and locked up in a box-room until I should be required. When I heard the door lock behind me, I lit a cigarette and began to test all the sensitive currents of my intuition in search of the meaning of this move. [...] My thoughts were interrupted by the opening of the door and in swept the Chief of the Paris Gestapo in full uniform. [...] "You are being sent back to England." [...] I was sure it was a trap and gaped at him in silent amazement. [...] "You're pulling my leg," I said, with a wry smile [...] "Not at all. You and a British major are being exchanged for a German lieutenant now in British hands. We are offering two of you to get him back." [...] Now I was sure it was a hoax. Why had he mooched around the room instead of bringing this out in the first place. [...] The Commander said: "I have to make certain that you don't escape in transit so two men will escort you to Berlin and the best method is to hand-cuff you". [...] "Why should I want to escape after what you told me about the exchange plan?" He gave me a knowing look and said, "Englishmen are crazy enough to escape on the last day of war and it is my duty to see that you reach Berlin."*[17]

---

17   Ibid, pp. 110-111-112-113.

This absorbing piece demonstrates the sharp acumen of Peter Churchill who, with a tricky question, embarrassed the Paris Gestapo Commander. For his part, the high officer replied with something unimpressive, and this confirmed the doubts in Churchill's mind. He would not be exchanged with anyone, but conducted to the Sachsenhausen Concentration Camp. The Gestapo tried to be friendly with him only to gather as much information as possible from their important prisoner, and Churchill understood it. He never talked.

Another interesting part to be mentioned under the label of "spy writing" is the description of the smart escape of some prisoners from the Sachsenhausen Concentration Camp, friends of Churchill. Many spy tricks would have been played on the camp guards so as not to be caught while they were digging a long underground tunnel necessary for their original escape. This piece of literature is truly engaging and it could have been seen as one of the inspirational sources which brought to the famous Hollywood movie, only nine years later: *The Great Escape.*[18]

> Soon after the arrival of "Wings" Dowse and Jimmy James, a leading article in the Deutsche Allgemeine Zeitung confirmed the rumour that about fifty of the seventy-eight men with whom they had escaped from Sagan had been shot after capture. [...] Instead of thanking their lucky stars that the mad rage of Hitler had somehow passed them by, it was precisely at this moment that they unanimously decided to show their captors to what extent they were cowed by this vile inhuman butchery, by escaping. All three and Johnny Dodge had been told by the S.S.

---

18 *The Great Escape* is a 1963 American World War II epic film starring Steve McQueen, James Garner, Richard Attenborough, and many other Hollywood stars. The movie describes in details the mass escape by British Commonwealth prisoners of war from a German POW camp through an underground self-made tunnel. Based on real events, it depicts a heavily fictionalised version of the escape with numerous compromises for its commercial appeal. Interesting is the fact that the director of the film has based one of the characters on Peter Churchill's prisoner friend Johnny Dodge, who was his room-mate in the Sachsenhausen Concentration Camp and who tried the tunnel escape, adding another clue to the inspirational theory of the book of Churchill for the famous movie. Moreover, Johnny Dodge, portrayed by the Hollywoodian actor Christopher Reeves, is the protagonist of *The Great Escape II: The Untold Story*, a 1988 American made-for-television action-adventure drama film and sequel to the original 1963 *The Great Escape* movie.

Officer who had escorted them to the camp that from Sonderlager "A"
there was simply no hope of escape. [...] Armed with this interesting
information they planned to make a tunnel from their hut which should
come out on the grass verge just outside the wall.[19]

These lines show and confirm us the fine ability of Churchill in
writing, and surely he would have been surprised when in 1963 the
famous movie came out, thinking that maybe the director had read
his work. Later on the book, Churchill describes all the details of the
building of the tunnel, as well as each member's escape, who will be
all captured again soon and re-sent to the same prisoners camp. He did
not take part in the escape and, although he was invited, he declined.

Figure 1. Identity card of *Pierre Chauvet* issued on 10th September 1940
(Simon Churchill's archive).

---

19   Ibid, p. 145.

Figures 2, 3, 4, 5. Some impressive images of Peter Churchill found in the
National Archives of Kew (UK) – (Ref. HS 9/314 – HS 9/315 – Personal Files
Peter Morland Churchill, 1939-1946) showing the typical look changes of a
secret agent.

8.4 *Dialogues, humour and sarcasm*

Definitely, one of the highlights of Churchill's writing is his
outstanding talent in using dialogues for his characters. For his first
three books, depicting his own experience during the conflict, it is
easy to think that maybe he invented or fictionalised most of the
dialogues. In fact, he wrote this works nearly ten years after the
real events and it would have been impossible for him to remember
perfectly what he or his friends exactly told each other. We have

the evidence that he kept a diary, which would have helped him in remembering all the details necessary to write down his stories, but his capturer, the German counter-espionage agent Colonel Henri, had seized it, and his owner never saw it again.[20] Surely, having kept it before facilitated his future memory, but in the end we are supposed to think that he almost fictionalised his fascinating dialogues that mark out his writing style.

The following long passage is an example of a simple interrogation carried out by the Camp Commandant, other officers and guards, asking Churchill information about his friends' escape through the tunnel, turns out to be a nice, fluent, and very detailed piece of prose:

> *"Captain Churchill, do you understand German?"*
> *"Yes," I replied.*
> *"Have you any idea why you have been called here?"*
> *"Certainly."*
> *"Why, then?"*
> *"Because of my friends' escape."*
> *"You knew about it then? From the very beginning? Did they ask you to go with them?"*
> *"Yes."*
> *"Why did you not go?"*
> *"Because I am not a prisoner of war, captured in uniform, whose escape is recognized by the Geneva Conventions."*
> *"I see," said the President, scratching his chin. Then looking at me sideways, he said.*
> *"If the gate was left open, would you go then?"*
> *"The gate would not improve my chances of not being recaptured."*
> *At this point a rather dull man at the far end of the table interrupted with,*
> *"But Captain Churchill, supposing the gate were opened and all the guards went away, would you go then?"*
> *Failing to understand what was in his mind, I smiled and said,*
> *"If the gate was opened and there was a rose arbour leading all the way to England with a pub at every milestone, I'd be out like a shot"*
> *The President stopped this nonsense with a point in my favour, by saying,*

---

20 *The only thing that Henri [...] had found was my diary [...]*, in Churchill Peter, *The Spirit in the Cage*, p. 10.

"Captain Churchill has already answered that question."

[...] "Captain, although of course we quite understand that these escapes are considered very sporting events amongst your compatriots, and we fully realize that you are not the kind of person who is going to give anything away that will help us recapture your friends, nevertheless there are one or two simple points we should like to clear up and perhaps you will help us with these. The first is, why did they go?"

"Because escaping is in their blood, and it is the duty of every British officer to escape."

"Yes, yes. I know all about that, but was there not some special reason? Were they badly treated here?"

[...] "They were treated perfectly well here. It was the classic escape, for the reasons I have already given."

[...] "Of course, we shall recapture your friends very soon, they haven't a chance."

Looking round at the dead-pan faces, I said somewhat quizzically, "I wonder."

I returned to my room highly delighted at the Gestapo's complete mystification over what was probably the only tunnel escape from an S.S. camp.[21]

This is one of the emblematic examples of the dialogues reported in his books and, as we have read, it helps us to understand distinctly how things really happened. Indeed, instead of giving us a short description of the facts, typical of war books or historical works, which are more descriptive and usually explain coldly the facts, Churchill normally prefers these kinds of truly effective dialogues.

A characteristic that often emerges from his dialogues is the use of humor and sarcasm, of course typical of British people, but very distinctive of Peter Churchill's personality. The very interesting detail about this feature, and baffling at the same time, is that he uses humor and sarcasm especially during complicated and sometimes dangerous situations, making his books even more exciting, compelling, and worthy of being read. A shining example of this dangerous behavior can be easily observed in these following lines, when he is, once more, interrogated, this time by an Italian

---

21   Churchill Peter, *The Spirit in the Cage*, pp. 155-156-157.

secret agent of the OVRA[22] after some days from his arrest and after having previously been beaten hard:

> *In a bleary daze I watched the OVRA man come in with a folder of papers. [...] I was just in the right mood for an interrogation.*
> *"Now do you feel like answering some questions?" he began weakly, without any preamble.*
> *"Go to Hell!" I said.*
> *He closed the dossier and got up.*
> *"I'll be back later."*
> *"You're wasting your time," I said. "Forget the paper work. The Germans will only do it all over again."*
> *"What makes you so sure we'll hand you over to the Germans?" he enquired, without much conviction.*
> *"It's pretty obvious, isn't it? They command and you obey."*
> *"We work on an equal footing."*
> *"And do your troops occupy Berlin as theirs occupy the whole of Italy?"*
> *"It is a reciprocal arrangement."*
> *"Go tell that to Mussolini," I growled.*
> *The wretched man who had merely had the i's of his previous shameful convictions dotted, shuffled dejectedly out of the cell.*[23]

One more time, here Churchill proves a high sense of sarcasm and has no fear of the consequences of his words, helped also by the fact that what he told to the OVRA man was just the reality of facts. However, the situation was certainly dangerous and critical, and even if the Churchill's words were depicting the evidence, they would have not prevented the Italian agent to act more severely on his prisoner.

The following lines, describing his reflection on his condition of a prisoner of war who could have risked death sentence, are a shining example of his humor and sarcasm even during tragic situations:

---

22 OVRA (Organizzazione per la Vigilanza e la Repressione dell'Antifascismo - "Organization for Vigilance and Repression of Anti-Fascism") was the Italian secret police during Benito Mussolini's Fascist regime.
23 Ibid, pp. 16-17.

> *It is one thing to sit over a pint of beer and discuss war as being*
> *natural recurring phenomena brought on for the reduction of an over-*
> *populated world. It is another to be caught up in the process of being*
> *reduced.*[24]

8.5 *Scientific and romantic prose*

The title of this paragraph could sound like a contradiction in
terms, but this is just how Peter Churchill has structured his writing
throughout his whole work. Particularly, this feature is what makes
his prose unique and recognizable, mixing up two opposite modes
of writing. Churchill was a secret agent and only for this reason
we can claim that he was a pragmatic man, who studied all his war
actions in every detail. When he later became a writer of novels,
he adopted the same course of action, scientifically studying and
preparing everything to be written down inside his works. Of
course, his writing evolved through the years and this is confirmed
also by the fact that his first fatigue, *Of Their Own Choice*, can be
considered his simplest and naked work under this point of view.
This book is the shortest of his personal trilogy and has only few
historical footnotes about people mentioned in the text. It will be
only with his second and third books that Churchill improved this
accurate characteristic, writing many historical and documental
footnotes regarding essentially every character, even minor's ones,
and producing a dense biographical index for *Duel of Wits* and a rich
"historical" appendix for *The Spirit in the Cage*. The biographical
index in *Duel of Wits* is a mere list of all the people named in the
book, showing a short description of what had been their destiny
during and after the war. Most of them were British secret agents,
French partisans, soldiers or officers of the British Army. This kind
of work should have been very difficult for the author, especially
because, at the time he wrote the book, all the files concerning the
secret missions and more generally the Second World War were
kept top-secret. So, tracing all the information described in this list
would have been a real challenge for Churchill who consigned to

---

24   Ibid, p. 87.

the audience of his time something very difficult to find at that time and even unbelievable for this genre. In the appendix of his third book, *The Spirit in the Cage*, the author goes far beyond from the simple list of his previous work. In addition to another list, he wrote eleven pages depicting what happened to these characters in details, giving to the reader a sort of interesting and touching continuing story for most of them. This kind of writing can be surely considered historical, like a documentary that gives us all the possible details of the story, providing us as much evidence as possible. In other passages of the same book, Churchill carries out this task with simple footnotes, referring to other author's historical books which could be helpful for his readers in deepen some facts or completing the story of a specific personality mentioned:

> *After a moving farewell to me and his other companions in the Movement, he went off alone into no-man's-land and blew himself up with a hand-grenade.* *[25]
> *(The footnote says: * "Offizieregegen Hitler" by Fabian von Schlabrendorff)*[26]

These lines demonstrate his true interest in studying deeply the subject of his works, showing us his desire to not leave anything to chance. In another example he describes a huge bombardment carried out by the allies not far from the concentration camp where he was held prisoner, and was able to personally witness it:

> *Half a dozen aircraft whined their way down to final destruction [...]. One parachute came down so close to our camp that we feared the man might land on the electrified wire, but whilst still half a mile up he swung away to fall onto the parade ground in the very centre of the S.S. camp. His fears may well be imagined as he saw the style of reception committee eagerly awaiting his descent. Nor were these fears unfounded, for in a War-Crimes Court after the war, an S.S. sergeant was condemned to die for kicking this man to death.*[27]

---

25 Churchill Peter, *The Spirit in the Cage*, p. 218.
26 Von Schlabrendorff Fabian und Von Gaevernitz Gero, *Offiziere gegen Hitler, nach einem Erlebnisbericht von Fabian v. Schlabrendorff*, Europa Verlag, Zürich, 1946.
27 Ibid, p. 170.

About this precise bombardment, Churchill undertook a serious research, finding out who was the Allied parachute man and his German murderer, which was the Crimes Court which judged him, and even anticipating us the destiny of the latter. These are only few lines, but being able to find all the information written in it shouldn't have been a minor effort for its author. Although he doesn't give us a footnote revealing the name of the protagonists, nor any details of this incredible action seen by his own eyes, he demonstrates us his will to investigate even the apparently insignificant element for his story.

Scientific writing is the other aspect of Churchill's work which can be associated with the historical one. In his first three books, the author meticulously reports maps of his movements during his secret missions[28] as well as frameworks and sketches regarding technical elements of it. In *Of Their Own Choice*, a detailed drawing concerning a plan of a flare-path is reported, with lines indicating the landing circuit for the plane, the necessary distance for a safe take-off, the right position of the signaling "lamp men", and even the wind direction.[29]

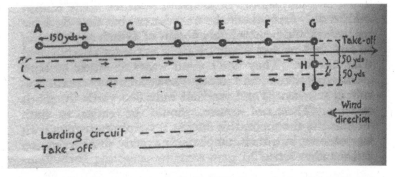

Figure 6. The drawing indicating all the details for a safe aircraft landing and subsequent take-off (*Of Their Own Choice* p. 122).

28   Maps concerning his and Odette movements appear in Churchill Peter, *Of Their Own Choice*, pp. 91-181, and *The Spirit in the Cage*, p.6.

29   Churchill Peter, *Of Their Own Choice*, Hodder and Stoughton, London, 1952, p. 122.

In his second book, *Duel of Wits*, Churchill draws two complicated and very specific sketches regarding his imminent sabotage mission to knock out an enemy radio station in Ste. Assise (F), indicating and describing it in all details.

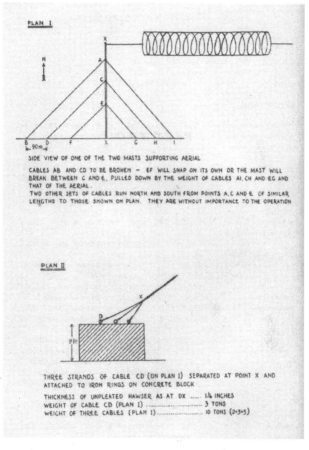

Figure 7. Sketches regarding a new sabotage mission to be carried out in the enemy radio station of Ste. Assise (*Duel of Wits*).

 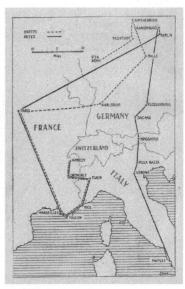

Figure 8, 9. Two detailed maps showing Peter Churchill's route in his first book *Of their Own Choice* (p. 91) and Peter and Odette routes in his third book *The Spirit in the Cage* (p. 6).

What emerges in contrast to Churchill's historical and scientific aspects of writing described until now is the remarkable poetic level and romanticism reached by some parts of his work. His academic studies and his love of world literature surely were the first causes that permitted him to produce very fine pieces of poetry hidden in his novels:

> *[...] the party was on the road to Basillac by 8 p.m., traversing the wooded countryside bathed in the light of a gigantic full moon. Whatever fate held in store for the quartet, they were not likely to forget the exquisite beauty of the ten kilometers' walk through that fairyland. Pale and black shafts of light stabbed downwards through the trees, lighting up the white patches of ground mist, like soft wads of cotton wool, as they formed here and there with the increasing cold of the bitter night. [...] Presently two heads came in sight bobbing up and*

down on two sets of shoulders that seemed to be floating towards them on top of the mist, as though walking through a gigantic foam bath.[30]

In these lines, the author describes us the long walk taken to reach a big flat field in the French countryside chosen for an imminent landing of a British aircraft. Instead of telling us that he, *Lise*, and his friends reached the field after a long walk, he proves us all his writing ability, describing the promenade as a fantastic dream in a fairyland.

The presence of his courier *Lise* during his activity as liaison officer for the French partisan movement, and the fact that he fell in love with her early on her arrival undoubtedly contributed to his romantic writing. Completely fool of her, and possessed by her love, Churchill writes truly romantic lines which contrast with his non-fiction historical books. The description of his arrival by parachute on the French alps, while *Lise* has prepared the bonfires and is waiting for him on a mountain top, expresses this feature very well:

Michel glided down, landing on his feet in the soft snow before her. He did not even have to bend his knees to take the shock. As they embraced each other at this crowning moment of their lives, the silk canopy fell lifeless on the snow and, in the crackling of the fire, he heard her sweet voice repeating his name, "Pierre, Pierre," in tones that told him everything a man could ever wish to hear.[31]

The fact that Churchill lived traumatic experiences during his captivity helped him as a cause of reflection. Also in this case, he is able to reach high poetic levels with his writing, just like the lines that follow, concerning the prisoners trapped in Fresnes penitentiary:

But in Fresnes the vast majority of prisoners had no idea how long they would be kept there or what to expect if they were sent to Germany, into the unknown terrors of the Concentration Camps. Like myself, therefore, they probably prepared themselves for the worst and then, when they had worked themselves into a state of almost happy acceptance of the thought that death would put an end to all their

---

30   Churchill Peter, *Duel of Wits*, p. 253.
31   Ibid, p. 309.

miseries, the sun would shine against their windows bringing back the passionate desire for life and the urgent hope that the cup of death was not for them. So came and went the resignation, the hope and the despair of the inmates of Fresnes, following each other round, hand in hand, like the four seasons, in a regular cycle.[32]

The romantic prose in *By Moonlight* deserves a separate paragraph. Being a work of fiction, it permitted its author to be much freer and inspired in this kind of composition, providing us real literary gems:

All the old enchantments, the turn of her head, the teasing smile, her trick of just touching the lobe of her ear with her long forefinger when she was searching for a word that eluded her, her voice [...].[33]

When he turned in, the lovely moon was flooding the yard, throwing each cobble into mountainous relief, and making deep dark valleys on the pantiled roof of the wheelwright's shop. A profound and ancient stillness filled the night. The sky was empty and infinitely distant. He gazed steadfastly until his eyes watered from weariness, then he turned abruptly away to his quiet bed.[34]
[...] and he'd be out of this place in two ticks and stepping elegantly into the gondola waiting for him outside. He would then glide stealthily along the canal – clean and freshly shaved – catch Christine in his arm as she threw herself off the bridge and go sailing off under a full moon into the black waters of Lake Annecy to the sounds of O Sole Mio while the thin curtains of the "Empire" closed over THE END and the customers filed out to the strains of the National Anthem – happy, exhausted and satisfied.[35]

8.6 *Cinema*

Peter Churchill was surely a cinema enthusiast, and this is proved by some passages in his novels where he mentions some of the films that have inspired him or that helped him understanding his

---

32   Churchill Peter, *The Spirit in the Cage*, p. 70.
33   Churchill Peter, *By Moonlight*, p. 26.
34   Ibid, p. 38.
35   Ibid, p. 154.

own experiences. In *Of their Own Choice,* he tells us that, before his first secret mission in France, he went to London and, after a detailed description of his route into the city, he continues (using third person) saying:

> *He hailed a taxi and gave the driver the name of a Leicester Square cinema. Leaving his case and mackintosh in the cloakroom, he bought himself the most expensive seat and settled down to three hours and forty minutes of "Gone with the Wind" [...].*[36]

In *The Spirit in the Cage,* Churchill is able to compare his current personal situation he is narrating to a specific movie scene, seen probably before war broke out. He is being interrogated in the Gestapo headquarters in Berlin by some officer:

> *I felt the eyes of all the officers on my left burning into me. I switched my glance across at them only to find their gaze averted. The whole picture reminded me of a scene from the film "Confessions of a Nazi Spy," the great difference being in the drab uniforms I now beheld and in the atmosphere created by the sullen fanaticism in the grey faces of the men around me.*[37]

The film mentioned is a 1939 classical American spy thriller, considered to be the first blatantly anti-Nazi film produced by a major Hollywood studio. Being a spy himself, Churchill unfortunately lived through the same terrifying experience he saw on the screen only few years before.

In another occasion, in the same novel, the author demonstrates his huge knowledge of world movies, this time mentioning a 1940 German propaganda film called *Feuertaufe* (Baptism of Fire), connecting it to the current situation of the war:

> *Hitler [...], ensconced in his Berlin bunker, was witnessing the relentless destruction of his capital. "Baptism of Fire", which had been his proud propaganda film to show any adversary what to expect from the Luftwaffe if they resisted his ambition for world power, was*

---

36   Churchill Peter, *Of Their Own Choice,* p. 42.
37   Churchill Peter, *The Spirit in the Cage,* p. 119.

catching up with him. The flames that he had spread around the world were now licking their way closer and closer to his bunker and his ears could pick up a faint grumble of crashing buildings that shook the very foundations of his underground lair.[38]

Churchill's familiarity with the world of cinema definitely ended up influencing also his composition. In fact, some specific narrative parts into his novels can be easily compared to a sort of movie screenplay, with all the characteristics and clichés typical of the cinema writing. One more time, descriptions and dialogues are his favourite subjects for this particular kind of writing:

> *"You come with me. I'm going to give Judd a big surprise."*
> *Putting the razor blade inside a breast pocket of my jacket I stalked out, closely followed by the two N.C.O.'s. Kicking in Judd's door I walked up to him. He remained seated at his table, pretending to read, a cigarette stuck out of the corner of his mouth.*
> *"What's the idea of refusing to obey my order?" I barked. Judd Ignored me. I got a hold of the front of his battle-dress with one hand and lifted him off his chair, saying, "Stand up when an officer speaks to you!"*
> *Judd leered at me, sure that he could get away with it, as usual. I smacked the cigarette out of his mouth, and gave him a stinging blow that sent him spinning into the corner of the room.*[39]

These lines are full of movie commonplaces, and here Churchill's narration is clearly affected by his high knowledge of how a good screenplay must be written. Everything recalls a movie scene: the razor blade put in his breast pocket, Churchill kicking the door, Judd pretending to read, his cigarette stuck out of the corner of his mouth. Moreover, the action, the movements, the postures, the timing, and finally Churchill smacking the cigarette out of Judd's mouth confirm this theory, reaching the highest point of it. There is no doubt that this particular passage is very cinematographic.

---

38   Ibid, p. 202.
39   Ibid, p. 161.

Finally, as a further example, the arrival of a new room-mate to the barrack of the concentration camp is an occasion for Churchill's composition to evoke another movie-like paragraph:

> *In the third week of March a giant Englishman was brought into my room, dressed in a rough suit which had clearly been fashioned from an airman's uniform. Slinging a bag off his shoulder he placed it apologetically on a chair, like a hiker entering a private room in a country pub who does not want to upset the person who may be snoozing beside the fire.*[40]

In *By Moonlight* there is a paragraph in which we can find both his spy and cinematographic writing, resuming in only few lines these two typical features:

> *He sauntered across to the other bus, asked the conductor when it was due to pull out and, hearing that there was a 20-minute wait, went off as casually as he could for a stroll towards the town. He preferred to get onto the bus when it was crowded, instead of immediately occupying a place where he could be scrutinised by all and sundry. With his hands thrust deep in his pockets he walked slowly round the square, away from the station, keeping the bus well in view. He noticed with relief that only people in civilian clothing were getting onto it.*
> *When he saw that there was standing room only he walked back, bought his ticket and took up his place in the central passage. He stood there with a look of assumed boredom while waiting for the bus to go. The seconds ticked away accompanied by the beating of his heart which felt strangely near his throat.*[41]

This typical cinematographic writing slows down the action, interspersing it with detailed and colourful descriptions of the situation and the feelings, creating a suspense to the narration, which can be compared to the distinctive traits of thriller or spy movie, definitely enriching Churchill's autobiographical or fiction-novels.

---

40   Ibid, pp. 141-142.
41   Churchill Peter, *By Moonlight*, p.134.

8.7 *Autobiographical elements in By Moonlight*

The fourth book of Peter Churchill, *By Moonlight*, deserves a particular analysis. It is in fact a mixture between fiction and real facts as the author specifies in a special note at the beginning:

> *This book is a work of fiction, but the background story of the Plateau de Glières is true in every detail. All the names that have been mentioned therein are the actual names of the men who lived this epic of the France Resistance, died as a result of it, or survived it.*[42]

The particular interest of Churchill about the Maquis de Glières French Resistance Group is due to the fact that he was the first British officer to discover and arm this group and, with his last secret mission, he was parachuted on Annecy, not far from their area. Unfortunately, he could not operate with them because he was soon betrayed and then captured by the German officer Colonel Henri. The only thing he was able to carry out before his capture was to drop them weapons, armaments, materials, and food, dealing also with the Secret Army of Faverges.

After having finished his personal trilogy, probably Churchill began to think what would have been if he had not been captured by the Germans, when he was dropped on the Maquis de Glières area. He probably had a bad taste in his mouth thinking about what he could have lived and done with these brave Frenchmen, so he thought about writing a work of fiction on "what might have been if...". The full story is based on a R.A.F. pilot of the Tempsford Squadron called Frank Bishop, who crashed with his aircraft on the mountains near the Plateau de Glières, after having dropped many containers full of weapons, food, etc., destined for the partisans of the Maquis. He saved himself and then decided to remain there and fight, shoulder to shoulder, with the local partisan. Since this point we can perceive the similarities with Peter Churchill's personal story. At the beginning of the second chapter, Frank, the protagonist of the novel, is described as follows:

---

42   Ibid, p. 7 (Special Note).

> *He was a lucky devil. All his life his stars had blessed him, and*
> *up to now he thought he had always been happy. Life have been*
> *full and exciting. His easy prowess at games, his gift for languages,*
> *both perfected at Cambridge, added to perfect health, and an affable*
> *disposition, had opened the most pleasing prospects to him. At twenty-*
> *one he had lived in Vienna, Budapest, and Stockholm, turning his*
> *tongue round the language, laughing and living in the sun.*[43]

The short description of the author for his protagonist is clearly based on his personal one, and many details are there to confirm it. Like Frank also Churchill had a happy and full young life, collecting noteworthy sport achievement with his university and then National team of Hockey, both have the gift of languages, being bilingual and studying it at Cambridge University, and finally Frank and Peter had grown up abroad, the former in Vienna, Budapest and Stockholm, the latter in Amsterdam, Stockholm, Milan, Palermo, and Algiers. Moreover, Frank is a R.A.F. pilot member of the Tempsford Squadron, the same Squadron that have dropped Churchill twice in France.

Chapter III gives us an important clue about another author's autobiographical element hidden into the text:

> *"The day's programme," said Mike, "will include a short trip to the*
> *coast of France, but not alas to the Côte-d'Azur…" […] Frank was not*
> *flying in the morning and he said "Cheerio" to Mike, clumping over to*
> *his plane […] The morning seemed endless.*
> *He was too long accustomed to it not to hear the distant note of the*
> *returning planes. Even now, no one was blasé about it.*
> *He went outside and counted them in. Then counted again. Four*
> *years had not lessened his reaction to this. Two missing, no, one*
> *laggard, limping through the darker cloud.*
> *He waited while they trooped in, to make their reports.*
> *He did not look for Mike.*
> *He heard the full story later. A lone fighter out of the sun, and a*
> *direct hit with a rocket shell. Mike's own tactics many times successful,*
> *but it happened to both sides, to the most vigilant, even to the most*
> *experienced. It was small comfort just than that the other had blasted*

---

43   Ibid, p. 16.

the attacker out of the sky. Out of them all, Mike had been the true happy warrior.

Mike, the pilot who falls in action in an air battle during a mission on the French coast, is no one else but the depiction of Walter Churchill, Peter's older brother, an "ace" pilot in the Royal Air Force during the war. The similarities are numerous and clear. In the summer of 1942, he was stationed in Malta as a group captain and, on 27th August, he was killed in action when his Spitfire V EP339 was hit by flak and crashed in flames while he was leading a raid on Biscari airfield near Gela in southern Sicily. We can suppose that Peter was very attached to his brother Walter and surely was thinking about him when he was creating Mike's character in this novel.

At the beginning of chapter VII, we have the crystalline confirmation that the author put his real personal experience in his fictional novel. In this passage, Frank asks information about the Maquis de Glières group to Pierre, one of his colleagues, and he replies:

"Well, we first heard this name from a British officer who discovered it quite accidentally when he was working in the Annecy area. I found out afterwards that it was I who had dropped this very man onto a snow-capped ledge over 5,000 feet up in the Alps."
"Good God! He must have been keen," said Frank.
"He was keen enough, all right, but the actual drop wasn't too bad because of the softness of the snow. The rear gunner watched him go down and land a few feet away from the bonfire which his friends had prepared as a signal for us. The sad part about the story is that this chap was picked up by the Gestapo a couple of days later and never managed to join up with the Maquis which he was responsible for arming [...]".[44]

These lines explain exactly what happened to Peter during his last mission even in the smallest details. Like the unlucky chap mentioned by Pierre, Peter was the first British officer who discovered and then armed the Maquis, while he was working in Annecy area, he also was dropped on a snowy mountain and he too risked to fall over

---

44   Ibid, p. 56.

the bonfires his friends had prepared as a signal. In addition, even Peter was picked up by the Gestapo soon later, and never managed to join up with the Maquis de Glières and fight with them. This short paragraph is really astonishing, not only it has resemblances to Churchill's real story, but it is depicting extremely well the final part of his last personal war mission. However, here the author is confusing the issue, because in this last example his personal story is no more referred to Frank, the protagonist of the novel, as before, but to another unnamed man in the plot, almost certainly a secret agent. In this way, the author tries to confuse his audience, mixing up and connecting his personal experience with more characters of his novel. Nonetheless, at the same time, Churchill is winking at his most faithful reader, which will discover and recognize all these particulars cleverly hided by the author.

At the end of the book, two other elements of the plot can be mentioned and easily connected to the personal experience of the author.

The first one is the final encounter between Frank and his beloved Christine, absolutely similar to Peter and Odette's one in the happy ending of *The Spirit in the Cage*, showing us one more time the author's high ability in a very detailed and passionate romantic writing:

> *As she stretched her hand to pick the flower, her slim fingers encircling the cold furry stem, she suddenly saw Frank in prison, dark and filthy, and desperate. A great oppressive blanket of fear and loathing pressed on her with an almost physical violence, and then she was free, standing up shaken and trembling.*
>
> *A step behind her on the path made her turn quickly.*
> *"Christine."*
> *She tried desperately, but no word came. She took a step forward, her fingers clenched around the flower as though to save herself. Then she was in his arms. Her face was drained of all colour, and her breath against his cheek was no more than the softest sigh. Frank put his arms around her and very gently they walked towards the house.*[45]
>
> *"Odette?" I whispered.*

---

45   Ibid, pp. 182-183.

"She's waiting for you in the office."
A film covered my eyes and my heart wept inside me. I heard no
more of what she said and sat in a numb daze until the car pulled up
outside the office. I walked up the stairs behind the others and waited
in a dream. [...] Seated at a table was a Major and opposite him, with
her left side towards me, sat Odette, in uniform, her hair resting on her
shoulders. She looked up. A smile came over her face and her mouth
half-opened.
    "Pierre!" she cried, rising from her chair and coming towards me as
I advanced with outstretched arms. So we remained in silence whilst the
door closed quietly behind us and we were alone.

The second element is the recognition received by both Frank and
Peter and done by the members of the Maquis de Glières after the
war.

Frank, eight years after the end of the conflict, did a pilgrimage
with Christine and his little son Michael to Annecy and on the
Plateau de Glières. Here he was very glad and surprised to find a
small stone monument with a French inscription that reported:

"IN HONOUR OF 'THE POPE', A BRAVE R.A.F. PILOT, WHO,
SINGLE-HANDED, LANDED HIS BURNING AIRCRAFT ON
THIS SPOT WITH ITS PRECIOUS LOAD OF ARMS, AND THEN
FOUGHT BESIDE US IN OUR BATTLE FOR FREEDOM."[46]

For his part, Churchill was decorated after the war at a private
Investiture held up in the mountains of the Haute Savoie by the
Departmental Commander of Resistance at the time of his story of
the Maquis. After this ceremony, he was so grateful that he began
researching about what happened to the partisans of the Maquis
de Glières after his own capture. In fact, in the *Acknowledgment*
of his book *By Moonlight*,[47] he declares that for all the facts and
basic material of the events depicted in his novel, he has to thank the
"Association des Réscapés de Glières", which produced the Glières
documentary published in France soon after the war. One more time,
here Churchill demonstrates one of his typical characteristics of

---

46   Ibid, p.187.
47   Ibid, p.8 (Acknowledgment).

writing, the scientific and historical writing, based on documenting himself accurately before writing something, and acting more as a historian than as a novelist.

8.8 *First and third person*

Peter Churchill wrote his first two books *Of their Own Choice* and *Duel of Wits* using the third person, and only with the last chapter of his personal trilogy, *The Spirit in the Cage*, he narrated in the first person. The Second World War had ended only nine years before Churchill published his first book, and the European political order was not definite yet. The future coalitions were not clear at that historical moment, and shortly after the world would have divided in two big parts, giving birth to two opposite poles, the communist and the capitalist one, generating the cold war. Writing novels concerning espionage or secret war's missions, was something still very delicate and even dangerous for the period. With regard to the British Intelligence, secret agents of the Special Operation Executive, as Churchill was, had to sign a specific document once they terminated their job and discharged. In this document, called "Official Secret Act", a non-disclosure-agreement between the secret service and its secret agents, it was declared that any agent would have not divulged any information concerning their secret war's missions, until this information would have not considered free by the Intelligence itself, normally fifty years after the end of the war. Surely, also Churchill signed this kind of document at the beginning of his career in the SOE, and that is why he sketched out his first two autobiographical novels disguising his true identity by using his codename (*Michel*). It is even true that his real identity is not well camouflaged because, between the lines, and in both novels, he reveals his actual surname several times, and later his complete name and rank.[48]

---

48   Churchill Peter, *Of Their Own Choice*, pp. 44…, and Churchill Peter, *Duel of Wits*, pp. 195…

Churchill's first two books were published in England by Hodder and Stoughton, London, in 1952 and 1953, narrating the plots in third person. Simultaneously he published the same works in the United States for G.P. Putnam's Sons, New York, but this time using first person narration. This choice was probably guided by the fear of the author of being prosecuted in some way by the British secret service regulations, which could have had complained about the fact that he did not observe their non-disclosure-agreement. This fact caused also a disagreement between Peter and his younger brother Oliver, he too a secret agent of the SOE with the rank of Major. Oliver had some resentment about Peter's publication of his SOE activities so soon after the war, when it was still considered a secret organisation and, from that point on, their relationship was distant. Moreover, there is also the question as to whether Oliver, among others, thought that Peter was exaggerating and glorifying what he and Odette had done during their war's missions, for self-publicity and to raise money for them both after the war.[49]

Instead, the third chapter of his trilogy, represented by the book *The Spirit in the Cage*, was written in the first person, both in the English and in the American version, possibly because it deals with his own captivity, after being captured by the German Colonel Henri, and after his real identity had already been revealed.

There is no record of Peter being prosecuted by the British Secret Services for having published books revealing important details of relatively recent secret war missions.

---

49   I was given this personal information by Simon Churchill, son of Major
     Oliver Churchill and nephew of Peter. This matter has been explained in detail
     in the chapter II, paragraph 2.10.

PART SIX

CONCLUSIONS

History and literature have always been the two main passions of my life. My historical research on an apparently unimportant diary of a partisan who lived in my same village allowed me to discover the magnificent figure of Captain Peter Churchill who, surprisingly, turned out to be also a fine novelist. His figure has been one of the most important in the British Intelligence during the Second World War, and he achieved also considerable success with his academic studies and with his personal sport career.

Having studied Churchill in depth as a historical figure, and knowing all the details of his war missions, thanks to all the documents found in the National Archives of Kew (UK), permitted me to understand very well his historical figure and his lead role in the British secret services during WWII. Moreover, having met some of his relatives, helped me understand accurately his personality and nature. Only after having finished the meticulous analysis of his figure, I became aware that I was lacking something about him. Knowing that he had written four novels, I understood that this was the missing piece. I was actually surprised when I found that all of his books could easily be bought online, although no one knew anything about them. But the biggest surprise came once I finished reading them. I was amazed, pleasantly shocked by the stories described, by the experiences, by the incredible plots and the fine writing style of the author. Finally, I understood that my understanding of Peter Churchill's figure was now complete and deserved more attention than it had received until that moment. So, I considered the idea of writing this dissertation, trying to describe and give value to the incredible literary production of Peter Churchill that, although its great success during the 1950s all over the world, was strangely forgotten shortly after, and never considered in academic studies anymore.

His first three books, *Of Their Own Choice* (1952), *Duel of Wits* (1953), and *The Spirit in the Cage* (1954), written in the short period of only three years, can be considered as a single long novel, or as a trilogy. These astonishing works full of action, courage, emotions, and even passion depict his personal experiences as a British SOE secret agent during the Second World War. Even if the first two books are in the third person, it is clear since the first pages that the protagonist is no other than the author. The reader gets immediately involved in the engaging plots and, thanks also to Churchill's simple, but not predictable writing, reading them is easy and engaging. In some parts of these three novels, it is easy to feel the author's emotions, his fears, his hopes, his doubts, and, when you least expect it, you find yourself in a small French village, in the middle of nowhere, trying to fool the German Gestapo and get a radio contact with London BBC headquarters.

The personal experiences lived and depicted by Churchill in his trilogy are so different and hard that it is quite difficult to understand how he could have faced all of them. Submarine trips, docking with a row felucca at night with stormy sea, walking for kilometers in the unknown countryside of a foreign country in winter and with heavy snow fall, hiding in a car boot to cross a state border, operating in the shadows with the enemy always breathing down your neck, being dropped by parachute in the mountains of Haute Savoie covered by the snow, being a prisoner for nearly two years and having been deported to some of the worst German concentration camps are only some of the incredible experiences lived by the author, who never glorifies himself for this. Writing his first two books in the third person and using his code-name, in fact, makes his stories less egotistical and perhaps a little more remote to the reader, though his writing style engages the reader with many interesting facts and twists in the storyline which keep us engaged. Moreover, the author provides a fascinating insight into the French Resistance movement and the activities of the Special Operations Executive in France, enriching the whole thing with detailed descriptions of the personalities involved. Being very perceptive about people's characteristics, easily understanding their strengths and weaknesses, the author has the ability of letting his readers feel they get to know the various people described in the books.

Finally, Churchill was fighting for the Allies during the war, but it doesn't mean that he could have not written these books neutrally, and the proof is that not all his enemies are portrayed as bad people. This is an almost unique feature for a book written only few years after the war ended: most of such books in fact depict the enemies as evil, never considering their points of view nor their emotions, and showing no mercy for them. In particular, Churchill praises a German priest, Paul Steinert, who visited him in prison many times, and a fellow prominent prisoner, Wehrmacht Colonel Bogislaw von Bonin, who intervened to protect the British and other foreign prisoners from their SS guards, when they were being transported away from Dachau Concentration Camp, when the American forces were advancing. Thanks to this particular characteristic, Churchill can be considered one of the pioneers of the new peaceful vision of the world, nowadays almost granted, but it must be considered the fact that, during the historical period when he was writing these novels, the Cold War was seriously raging.

The fourth novel by Churchill analysed in this thesis is a work of fiction, although the background story is true in every detail. Here the author shows his uncommon ability in inventing a plot on a true background story, thanks to his personal life experiences. In fact, *By Moonlight* (1958) tells the story of a British R.A.F. pilot who fought with a French partisan group called Maquis de Glières, and who lived almost the same adventures of Peter Churchill. The success and the beauty of this novel lie, indeed, in its plausibility, which renders it a real charming example of a classic war fiction.

All of Churchill's works are also very interesting from a literary point of view because they mix many literary genres. His personal trilogy can surely be connected and compared with the non-fiction novel, with the so-called faction, with memoirs and autobiographical novels, but mostly they are war and spy novels, depicting the true experiences of the author, who reaches high literary peaks bearing witness to his traumatic past. His fourth fiction novel must obviously be considered separately, but even this one has the characteristic of mixing different literary genres. Being a fictional work, it is a war fiction novel, however, it also includes true historical facts and details, particularly Churchill's biographical elements, which make it a credible full-fledged historical war novel.

Peter Churchill definitely lived an incredible life, being that kind of person that was successful in everything he undertook, a kind of King Midas, turning everything he touched into gold. The son of a consul, he had the opportunity to travel around the world, learning many different languages and cultures. He studied in Cambridge, one of the most prestigious Universities in the world, he reached unbelievable goals with his sport career, and finally he is considered one of the leading figures of the British intelligence during the Second World War. However, all this was not enough for him and, after the war, he became a fine novelist reaching, together with his war and life companion Odette, huge fame thanks to his excellent novels. The figures of Peter and his wife were also portrayed in the movie *Odette*, famous worldwide, whose premiere was attended by King George VI and his wife the Queen. The fact that his novels have since been forgotten does not mean that they have lost their literary value and relevance: time can be an enemy sometimes, and it is for this precise reason that I decided to "bring back to light" the story of an incredible personality, Captain Peter Churchill, but above all his marvelous forgotten novels.

APPENDIX

ABOUT THE CHURCHILL FAMILY

Peter Churchill was the middle of three brothers, each of whom had an outstanding career during World War II, and each of whom was awarded the *Distinguished Service Order (DSO)*, the second highest military award in Britain, and also a second high-level medal of gallantry. It is not known if any other family had brothers who were similarly highly decorated.

Their father served as a British Consul and each of the brothers was born in Europe: Walter, the oldest, and Peter were born in Amsterdam, while the youngest, Oliver, was born in Stockholm. They grew up in various European countries though all were educated in England.

In this last part of the book, I tried to trace a short biography of the Churchill family and of Peter's two brothers who, like him, served with distinction during World War II. In doing this I have been flanked and helped by my friend Simon Churchill, Peter's nephew, son of Peter's brother Oliver, who, together with me, wrote all the Wikipedia's pages about his family, his father and his two uncles.

10.1 *William Nosworthy Churchill and his son Henry Adrian*

The great-grandfather of the three brothers was William Nosworthy Churchill (1796-1846), a British-born journalist who moved to Turkey aged 19. He worked as a translator at the American Consulate in Constantinople and founded the first private newspaper.[1] One of his sons, Henry Adrian Churchill (1828 –1886),

---

1   *Ceride-i Havadis* (Journal of News) was the first semi-official newspaper in the Ottoman Empire, and was published from 1840 to 1877.

was an archaeological explorer of ancient Mesopotamia and a British diplomat who stopped much of the commercial slavery in Zanzibar and helped prevent a war between Zanzibar and Oman. Born in Adrianople (modern day Edirne) in Turkish Thrace, he married Maria Braniefska and had seven children, four of whom followed him into the diplomatic service. Following his archaeological explorations in the desert and marshes of Chaldaea from the Euphrates to the lower Tigris, he became an Arabic translator to Colonel Atwell Lake and took part in the defence of Kars during which he became a prisoner of the Russians. From the age of 26 he worked in the British Diplomatic Service and was appointed British Consul in Sarajevo, Bosnia; Jassy, Romania; Moldavia; Syria; Algeria; Zanzibar, Resht, Persia; and finally Palermo, Sicily, where he died in office in 1886 aged 57. He was a proficient artist and an accomplished watercolourist and during his travels he produced extensive detailed drawings and sketches, which were subsequently deposited in the British Museum and the Geological Society in London.

Figure 1. Henry Adrian Churchill.

10.2 *William Algernon Churchill*

One of the sons of Henry Adrian, William Algernon Churchill, was born in Algiers in 1865and married Hannah Violet Myers whose sister married his brother Sydney. They had four children: Walter (1907–1942), Peter (1909–1972), Flora (1911–1929), and Oliver (1914–1997). In 1891, William was appointed British Vice-Consul in Mozambique, then Consul in Mozambique; Pará, Amazon Provinces, Brazil; Amsterdam; Stockholm; and finally Consul-General in Milan in 1919, retiring in 1922 to live in Malvern, Worcestershire. During retirement, he served as Acting Consul in Palermo for 3 months in 1928, and in Algiers from 1934 to 1936. William was also an art historian with particular interest in watermarks in paper. He was the author of what is still the standard reference work on early European paper and papermaking, *Watermarks in Paper in Holland, England, France, etc., in the XVII and XVIII centuries, and their interconnection*, first published in 1935. This book is still in print.

The extensive introduction contains inter alia an alphabetical List of Dutch papermakers, a list of French paper-makers who worked for the Dutch market, and a list of British paper-makers and mills. At the end a survey of particulars concerning the watermarks in question. The corpus of the work is systematically arranged according to motives and contains 578 full-size reproductions of watermarks. With illustrations and 578 facsimiles of watermarks.[2]

In 1936, William donated a large collection of dated watermarks, ranging from the 15th to the 19th Centuries, to the Department of Manuscripts at the British Museum in London. William died on 23rd December 1947 after having lost one of his three boys who fought for their Country in the Second World War.

---

2   Description in *Amazon Books*.

Figure 2. The art historian and British diplomat William Algernon Churchill,
father of Walter, Peter, and Oliver.

10.3 *Walter Myers Churchill*

Figure 3. A young Walter Churchill.

Walter Myers Churchill was born on 24th November 1907 in Amsterdam and was named after his uncle Walter Myers, an eminent physician and bacteriologist who died in 1901 aged 28 in Brazil while studying the transmission of yellow fever. He was educated at Sedbergh School and in 1926 he read Modern Languages at King's College, Cambridge. He then became an aeronautical engineer with Armstrong Siddeley Motors, Coventry, after which he started an aviation precision engineering company, Churchill Components (Coventry) Ltd, in 1937, which supplied machined parts such as exhaust valves for radial aero-engines to Armstrong Siddeley. Coventry was a city renowned for its motor industry and precision engineering and was targeted by the Luftwaffe early in the war who blitzed the city in 1941, after which Walter re-located the company to Market Bosworth, a small rural town 45 km north-west of Birmingham away from the attention of German aircraft. The company machined compressor blades for the gas-turbine engines developed by Sir Frank Whittle, the jet-engine pioneer in the early 1940s. Walter joined the Auxiliary Air Force in 1932 as a pilot officer and appointed to No. 605 (County of Warwick) Squadron. He was promoted to flight Lieutenant in June 1937 and transferred from the AAF to the Auxiliary Air Force Reserve of Officers in January 1939. He was recalled to No. 605 Squadron and full-time service in August 1939 and commanded the squadron from June to September 1940, when he was succeeded by Archie McKellar. Churchill later served with No. 3 Squadron and No. 71 (Eagle) Squadron and took part in the Battle of Britain as a squadron leader. He was then promoted to Wing Commander, then Group Captain. During his tenure as Squadron Commander with 71 (Eagle) at R.A.F. Debden, he instructed his pilots to land the outdated Brewster Buffaloes with their tail wheels unlocked, causing damage to the aircraft after which Hurricanes were issued to the squadron.

Figure 4. 605 Squadron in front of a biplane fighter/bomber. Walter Churchill is the third from the left.

Walter became an 'ace' pilot credited with seven «kills», and was awarded a Distinguished Service Order and a Distinguished Flying

Cross. Here we can read the reason for these two-awarding appeared on *The London Gazette* n. 34860 on 31st May 1940 (page 3252):

> *31 May 1940: Flight Lieutenant Walter Myers Churchill is awarded the Distinguished Flying Cross:*
> *This officer has shot down three enemy aircraft since his arrival in France and has led many patrols with courage and skill.*

> *31 May 1940: Flight Lieutenant Walter Myers Churchill DFC (90241) is appointed a Companion of the Distinguished Service Order:*
> *This officer assumed command of a squadron shortly after its arrival in France and led it with marked success, inspiring his pilots and maintenance crews magnificently. He undertook the tactical instruction of new pilots, led many patrols successfully and organised his ground defences and crews in an exemplary manner. While under his command the squadron destroyed 62 enemy aircraft and he was throughout the main-spring of the offensive spirit, their excellent tactics and their adequate maintenance results. Only four pilots of the squadron were lost. Flight Lieutenant Churchill has recently destroyed four enemy aircraft, bringing his total to seven.*

In addition to this, Walter evaluated various makes of fighter aircraft for the R.A.F. and played a key role in getting Spitfire aircraft to the defence of Malta. In August 1942, he was stationed in Malta as a Group Captain. Prior to the Allied landings in Sicily, attacks were made on German airfields, and on 27th August 1942 he led a raid in a Spitfire on Biscari airfield near Gela in southern Sicily during which he was shot down and killed in action. He was buried at the Syracuse War Cemetery where he is the highest-ranking officer to be interred.

Figure 5. Gravestone of Group Captain Walter Myers Churchill at Syracuse War Cemetery in Sicily (I).

Following Walter's death, Air Vice Marshal Sir Keith Rodney Park,[3] Air Officer Commanding, R.A.F. Mediterranean, wrote this letter to his widow Joyce (Hartley) Churchill:

---

3   Air Chief Marshal Sir Keith Rodney Park, (15 June 1892 - 6 February 1975) was a highly decorated New Zealander who served as a senior R.A.F. officer during WWI and WWII.

By 1st Air Mail

a.o.c.
Headquarters,
R.A.F. Mediterranean.
28th. August, 1942.

Reference:
HQMED/489/1044/DO.

Dear Mrs. Churchill,

I am writing because I feel that it may be some comfort to you in your great loss to know that your husband met his end leading a fighter formation in a most successful attack on the enemy. Though Walter Churchill has passed on, his fine example and inspired leadership will live on in Malta to the end of the war. He arrived in Malta leading a formation of reinforcing Spitfires to protect the last vitally important convoy. During his all too short stay in Malta, Walter Churchill was an inspiration to the fighter Squadrons in the air and on the ground.

I have talked to the pilots who were flying next to your husband during his last fighter sweep and it may comfort you a little to know that his end must have been almost instantaneous because his aircraft appeared to get one unlucky direct hit from an anti-aircraft shell.

If it was ordained that Walter Churchill was to give his life for his country, I feel sure he would have chosen to end as he did, leading a fighter formation on a daring and most successful fighter sweep over enemy territory. All of us here feel his loss very deeply, and we send you our most sincere sympathy.

Yours very sincerely
K. R. Park[4]

---

4   The letter is from the archive of James Churchill, son of Walter.

After the war, Churchill Components (Coventry) Ltd continued under the management of his wife, Joyce, and subsequently that of his second son, James. The company is now known as J. J. Churchill Ltd. and is managed by James's son, Andrew.

Figure 6. Joyce Churchill.

10.4 *William Oliver Churchill*

Figure 7. William Oliver Churchill during his service in the SOE.
The National Archives, Kew (UK) – Ref. n. HS 9/316/3.

As I wrote in the very first part of the book regarding my research, the first clue about "a Churchill" in my area during the Resistance period was the presence, among a group of partisans of my village, of a certain *Mr. Antonio* who, after many investigations, turned out to be William Oliver Churchill, the youngest brother of Peter, son of my future dear friend Simon Churchill. About Oliver, in 2018, I wrote a historical essay for the Catholic University of the Sacred Heart of Brescia called: "La missione alleata Fairway: Un Churchill in Valle Camonica"[5] (The Allied Mission Fairway: a Churchill in the Camonica Valley) and here below I am reporting the main parts of it which describe the figure and the life of Major Oliver Churchill.

William Oliver Churchill was born in Stockholm on 11th October 1914, son of William Algernon, the British Consul in Sweden at the time. In the early years of his life, thanks to his father's job, he spent a few years in Milan and then in Algiers, where he was able to learn the languages and traditions of both countries. His father definitely returned to England when Oliver was about 14 years old and firstly settled near Buckingham. After having moved, Oliver spent his youth in the small town of Cambridge, where he passionately studied modern languages at King's College and subsequently enrolled in the Faculty of Architecture at the local University. In the meantime, the outbreak of the Second World War shook the world and Oliver's life as well and, because of this tragic event, he had to interrupt his studies.

Just shortly before the start of the conflict, perhaps anticipating the course of events, Oliver volunteered for the Territorial Army on 5th August 1939. He began his military life as a second Lieutenant in the 10th Battalion of the Worcestershire Regiment, where he remained for about two years, carrying out very simple and humble tasks. In October 1941, perhaps having demonstrated suitable features, he was transferred to Arisaig in Scotland, where he took part in some paramilitary training for future SOE officers. This formation included physical training in preparation for parachuting, reading and using a compass, topography, intelligence methods, communications, use of weapons, report writing and silent killing methods. Then, from November 1941 and for about a month, Oliver began a tough training that took him to various locations in England such as Beaulieu and Manchester. Finally, he reached Limavady, County Londonderry, Northern Ireland, where he undertook his first proper parachute jumps. After a few weeks, he was transferred to Malta by sea, where he remained for about 6 months, continuing

---

5   "La missione alleata Fairway: Un Churchill in Valle Camonica" in *Gli Alleati a Brescia tra guerra e ricostruzione - Fonti, ricerche, interpretazioni*, edited by Rolando Anni, Giovanni Gregorini, Maria Paola Pasini, FrancoAngeli Edizioni, Milano, 2018, pp.135-154.

to train and commanding a small group of recruits. Between the summer of 1942 and September 1943, Oliver participated in many other paramilitary and parachute trainings, increasingly harder and more specific, eventually becoming an instructor. During this time, he was transferred to various locations around the Mediterranean, firstly to Haifa, then to Kabrit in Egypt, Jerusalem, Cairo, Turkey and Cyprus, where he had the opportunity to come into contact with several Italian soldiers in the various British prison camps.

It was only in September 1943, after two years of hard training and having acquired the rank of Captain, that Oliver took part in his first real war mission as a secret agent of the Special Operation Executive: Operation Acheron.

After the Italian armistice signed with the Allies on 8th September 1943, the American General Eisenhower considered the Greek island of Corfu as strategic for the Balkan campaign and decided to immediately send a mission to the Italian troop command located on the island. The Germans, however, of the same opinion, invaded the island on 14th September. The purpose of the mission was to get in touch with the Italian troop command and to explain the Allied intentions, trying to reassure the Italians that new reinforcements were being sent. Oliver and radio operator Harrison were parachuted onto the island at 4.15 a.m. on 21st September 1943, only two weeks after the armistice and one week after the German invasion of the island. Confusion was great during the days immediately following the armistice, also caused by poor communications; the next passage about the arrival on the island, written by Churchill in his report at the end of the mission, can be clarifying in this sense:

> *Little was known of the situation in Corfu. Fighting was to be expected anywhere. You might be fired-on by either or both sides.*

Not without problems, they tracked down Colonel Luigi Lusignani of the 18th Infantry Regiment of the Acqui Division. They immediately informed him that the Allied intentions were to fully support the Italian Army and asked the Colonel to resist until the imminent arrival of new Allied troops. Unfortunately, however, they were unable to inform the SOE headquarters in Cairo about the situation on the island at that time. During the drop, the parachute where the spare batteries for the radio transmitter were attached failed to open so, after the impact with the ground, they resulted unusable. Initially there was a radio contact, but shortly afterwards the radio stopped working permanently as the only batteries available were exhausted, thus preventing Churchill and the radio operator from transmitting and receiving important instructions. In the meantime, several German air raids began to devastate the entire island and on 25th September, after realising the imminent arrival of numerous German reinforcements, Churchill and Harrison decided to leave Corfu. However, they hid for a few more days, disguised as civilians in various villages, while most of the Italian troops and officers, including Colonel Lusignani, were captured and executed by the Germans. It was only after a few days in the bush that Churchill and his companion managed to find a real possibility of escaping from the island, thanks to a seventy-year-old local man. On a small motorboat, driven by three Italian civilians and together with eleven fleeing soldiers and sailors, Churchill and Harrison left the village of Palaiokastritsa and reached the islands of Mathraki, Ereikoussa, and Fano at night, en route to Italy. Oliver's description of the three sailors of the small boat is interesting and not very comforting:

One dotard, one drunkard and the father of a thief.

The following night, the small boat reached the Italian coast, but due to a sudden change in the wind it did not reach Otranto as planned, but an unspecified location in the Gulf of Taranto. Having realised their mistake, after about five hours, the boat was able to land in Otranto. This is what Oliver wrote in his report about the troubled voyage:

By first light we saw land. But for one of the Italian sailors from Corfu, the captain would have turned about. He did not recognize the coast, and thought we had sailed in a circle and were off Albania. The captain was too bleary-eyed to read the compass and the boson helpless with the sails. All this the sailors saw too, as well as keeping the mechanic at the pumps. Our sailor saw that we were in the Bay of Taranto. The drift had carried us five hours off our course.

Once in Otranto, Churchill and his companion reached SOE headquarters in Brindisi, where they were debriefed and questioned by Major De Haan about their mission. Then, after receiving further instructions from No. 1 Special Force Commander Holdsworth, on 18th October they both flew to Catania and then, by sea, returned to the SOE headquarters in Cairo.

Amongst the mission papers found in the Kew archives, a document dated 23rd September 1943 indicated that Captain Churchill and his radio operator Harrison had possibly died in battle and they were reported Missing in Action. This was probably deduced from the fact that, after the first radio contacts, all communication with the mission had been completely cut off. Having also learned of the tragic events that had occurred to the Italian Army on the island, British Intelligence considered both of its men fallen into enemy hands and, consequently, shot. It was only when Churchill and Harrison reached Cairo at 9.30 p.m. on 21st October that the news of their deaths was happily rectified.

Thanks also to the *Acheron* mission, Corfu was finally liberated and occupied by the 40th Commando of the British Royal Navy, which landed on the island on 14th October of that same year, unfortunately too late to avoid the famous massacres of Corfu and Cephalonia, perpetrated by German troops. Between the end of October '43 and June '44, Churchill remained in the western Mediterranean at various commands, being awarded, on 17th February 1944, the Military Cross for valour shown during *Operation Acheron*.

In early June 1944, after further training, Captain Churchill was transferred to a location called Maryland, code-name for the SOE headquarters in southern Italy, located near Brindisi. Here, he was informed about a new mission to be carried out in northern Italy, in Val d'Aosta, some 50 km north of Turin, called *Operation Nunnery*. The purpose of this mission was to establish a link between the local partisan command and the Allies, for future launches of food, weapons and supplies to the various local formations. The records in the National Archives at Kew include a description of the aims and tasks to be carried out, but there is no record it took place and may have been cancelled due to poor weather preventing a parachute drop, or due to changing priorities since Oliver was soon assigned to another operation in northern Italy. Even the documents drawn up by Churchill at the end of the war, in which he summarised his long activities as a British secret agent, make no mention of *Operation Nunnery*.

In the meantime, SOE headquarters and CLNAI were planning a new mission together that would have soon involved Oliver. On 25th June 1944, General Raffaele Cadorna Jr.[6] received a brief radiogram through a staff officer:

> *Comitato di Liberazione Alta Italia chiede l'assegnazione, in veste di consigliere militare, del generale Raffaele Cadorna, il quale gode sua piena fiducia.*[7]

In addition, the communiqué continued, his acceptance was needed for a personal mission in the north of Italy. Without any hesitation, Cadorna accepted. A few days later, the General visited the Special Force headquarters installed in Rome, in Via Oriani, where he met several British officers and agents who, once again, asked him if he was really interested in participating in the mission described above. Cadorna accepted a second time. After having initially moved to Monopoli, towards the end of July he reached the airfield of Brindisi where he was welcomed by Captain Beauky, administrative director of the Special Force. There he met Captain W. Oliver Churchill, who would soon be joining him on his next mission. The General immediately had a good impression of the British officer, describing him as a fine young man of admirable behaviour. After a few days of training in the field and several parachute jumps, Cadorna and Churchill went to Rome to visit Marshal Alexander who, unfortunately, was absent in those days, as

---

6   Raffaele Cadorna Jr. (Pallanza, 12 September 1889 - Verbania, 20 December 1973) was the son of the famous General Luigi Cadorna, chief of staff of the Italian Army during the First World War, and grandson of Raffaele, commander of the Italian troops in the taking of Rome (20 September 1870). He was in charge of organising the Resistance against the German occupation forces and, in July 1944, took command of the "Corpo Volontari della Libertà", coordinating the military strategy of the Resistance.

7   "Comitato di Liberazione Alta Italia (Upper Italy Liberation Committee) asked for the assignment of General Raffaele Cadorna as military adviser, who enjoyed his full confidence" (my translation).

he was busy accompanying King George of England, who had come to Italy to inspect the British troops. On 3rd August, they returned to Puglia, this time to Bari, waiting for the availability of an aircraft. All the details of the new forthcoming mission, which took the name *Operation Floodlight/Fairway*, were now in place. However, they had to wait about a week for an aircraft and only on 11th August, the two officers were informed about their imminent departure. On that day, Major De Hahn told them that they would have been dropped to Cavallina Valley, in the province of Bergamo, and arrangements for a proper reception had been made with a local partisan band, responsible for lighting signal fires. The directives, given by the Special Force command, were as follows:

> *Dopo l'arrivo in Val Cavallina, trasferirsi e stabilirsi quanto prima in Valle Camonica, prendendo subito contatto col CLNAI.*[8]

The Camonica Valley, according to SOE information, was considered a free zone, because it was occupied by a local well-trained partisan formation called *Fiamme Verdi* (Green Flames). SOE also promised the General and the members of the mission the widest possible support to encourage military action but, at the same time, threatened to suspend this support if the military action would have been disturbed by political interference.[9] These directives were also accompanied by a well-wishing letter from the British Marshal Harold Alexander.[10]

---

8   "After arriving in Cavallina Valley, move and settle in Camonica Valley as soon as possible, immediately making contact with the CLNAI" (my translation).

9   In fact, the Allies preferred to deal with apolitical, autonomous and Catholic commands rather than with the G. L. (Giustizia e Libertà) and Garibaldini groups.

10 *HEADQUARTERS*
    Allied Forces in Italy, C.M.P.   *3 August 1944*
    Dear ***
    I am very sorry that I was not here when you visited this command two days ago, but I am pleased to learn from General Harding that you had a very constructive talk.
    I take this opportunity of thanking you for accepting this very difficult and dangerous action in the North and of wishing you every success.

Back to Brindisi, Churchill and Cadorna met Captain Beauky and were finally equipped. Amongst the various pieces of luggage, they were bundled up with two million lire in cash, one each. However, finding it impossible to stuff themselves with so much paper, they decided to keep only half a million each and parachute the remainder boxed with the rest of the equipment. Shortly afterwards, they met the other members of the mission, Mr. Augusto de Laurentiis, an officer of the Ministry of Finance close to the Action Party (code-names: *Mario Mazzei, Augusto Ferreo*), and wireless operator Sergeant Nicola delle Monache (code-names: *Alfieri, Alf del Magro*), who was carrying two radios and a small generator. Churchill and Cadorna had code names too: *Amalfi Giacomo* and *Curti Ricci Carlo* for the former and *Anthony (Antonio) Peters* for the latter. In the meantime, from the beginning of July, the messages between the SOE headquarters in Bern, Switzerland, and the radio located on the bell tower in Cividate Camuno in the Camonica Valley began to intensify. Intense correspondence of clandestine telegraphic messages also contributed to facilitate the communication between the two sides. Here we can read the most important passages:

23 July 1944:
General Fiori at Supreme Command Alt–General should come immediately Alt– C.L.N. is waiting for General Cadorna to coordinate and organise the North Italian Command Alt -...

26 July 1944 – Important Message:
To Gen. Fiori Alt – we are ready to launch first unit of Cadorna mission Alt – we urgently need an identified launch field where men could be received Alt - ...

When you meet with the leaders of the Regional Organisations, please be so kind as to convey to them my thanks for their excellent achievements and to assure them that we will continue to support their efforts to the fullest extent that we are able.
While we shall continue to provide supplies and call for specific action by the usual means, I shall look forward to receiving communications from you regarding the general situation in the North, together with an indication of the best way in which we may assist you.
I wish you all the best of luck, dear ***, and hope that we may meet under more peaceful conditions in the not-too-distant future.
Yours H. R. Alexander General Commander-in-Chief

30 July 1944 – Following message is sent:
Launch fields ready Alt – field called Alberino 6 suitable for isolated
men or groups launch Alt – ready every night Alt – Negative message:
Sparrow flies – Positive: Horses of the sun - ...

4 August 1944:
The message indicating the forthcoming arrival of a British mission
is repeated; Cadorna, a British officer and a radio operator.

6 August 1944:
A few hope to launch field I bis this moon due to bad position in
high mountain Alt – Be ready with field I bis but in the meantime try to
arrange another field in a plain to be able to receive Cadorna mission,
consisting in 4 men and 4 boxes Alt – We suggest on the south bank of
Iseo Lake in the area of Monte Alto and Monte Griveccino Alt - ...

8 August 1944:
Field Alberino I-bis has been clear and with no clouds for three
nights. Waiting mission's launch during this moon after midnight Alt
- ...

Before leaving, Captain Churchill was promoted to the rank of Major. On 11th August 1944, at 23:00, the four members of the mission, with their parachutes and suits, climbed into a four-engine Halifax aircraft, which slowly took off and turned north-west. The aircraft took a long time to reach its goal. Being without any defensive armament it did not follow a direct route in order to avoid any unpleasant encounters. The members of the mission took the opportunity to sleep a bit. Around 2 a.m., on the morning of 12th August, the big bomber finally reached the skies over Cavallina Valley and the four men parachuted down in the darkness, only illuminated by the signal fires prepared by the partisans. Unfortunately, after a near-perfect jump, Cadorna and Churchill fell abruptly to the ground and, due to a violent impact with the ground, both suffered some wounds and bruises, Churchill spraining his ankle. The pilot had signalled their launch too early, so that they landed on the sloping, rocky banks near a small mountain lake, instead of on a richly moss-covered hill as planned. All four landed on the slopes of Mount Sparavera, in Botta Alta, in the municipality of Ranzanico. They were immediately met by the leader of the local partisan group who, together with his men, tried to collect all the 'luggage' parachuted, and, advising them to leave the area as soon as possible, he sent them to their future accommodation. The group then reached a large house in a secluded spot outside the village, but after a few minutes' rest, alerted by a runner to an imminent round-up by some divisions of fascist soldiers, they all had to find temporary shelter in the surrounding woods. After a couple of hours' march, they reached the bottom of the valley and settled in the house of the partisan commander called Costante Federici, who declared that he was a member of the Green Flames.[11]

Figure 8. Monument and commemorative plaque on Mount Sparavera in Ranzanico (I), where Oliver Churchill and all the members of the Allied Fairway Mission were dropped in the night of 12th August 1944.

---

11   Actually, Costante Federici was the head of the Nullo Brigade of G. L., which had previously been contacted by the command of the Tito Speri Division of the Green Flames of Camonica Valley, to be incorporated into its ranks. At that moment his brigade had to follow the operative directives of the Tito Speri but the official passage to the Fiamme Verdi never took place and this caused unpleasant consequences for the Cadorna mission, as well as showing the lack of seriousness and low influence of the commanders of the Nullo on their men. Even Cadorna himself did not have a good impression of them: "They were mostly young men who had come to escape from military service or from work. The formation was lacking in armament, equipment and training, but above all it did not have a stable logistic base for provisions". (Raffaele Cadorna Jr. *La Riscossa: La testimonianza del generale dei partigiani con documenti inediti*, Bietti, Milano, 1977, p. 107).

Once the night had passed, the partisans were very unhappy to know that the containers dropped by the mission did not contain any weapons or ammunition, equipment they had been impatiently waiting for. They also stated that, after recovering the material from the drop, they were forced to abandon part of the precious cargo on the spot, due to the ongoing fascist round-up. After coming back to the site to retrieve it, however, they were unpleasantly surprised to find only a few boxes, noting the disappearance of others, containing various important equipment and, especially, the other million lire.[12] Churchill was furious, among the looted materials there were also his civilian clothes. De Laurentis, on the other hand, was desperate for the disappearance of a Bible, a precious and traditional object in Waldensian families, such as his own.

Actually, there was a round-up on Mount Sparavera on the night between 11th and 12th August 1944. Here we can read some parts of the report of the action, written by Lieutenant Massimo Guzzini of the O.P. "Macerata" Company stationed in Clusone, which turns out to be very accurate and full of interesting details:

Following verbal orders received from the Commander of the O.P. "Macerata" Company Captain Antonelli, the night of 11/8, at 2:30am a department under the command of the undersigned left to Endine to participate in a round-up action in the area between Endine and Gandino together with O.P. Company of Bergamo and the German S.S [...] When we reached Mount Sparavera [...] the vanguard and then almost the whole column were hit by a violent fire of automatic weapons placed on the mountainside. With a rapid manoeuvre [...] the whole unit lined up in combat order facing the enemy. For a few seconds there was an incessant hissing of bullets above our heads. Immediately our reaction began [...] As soon as the machine gun started firing [...] the rebels retreated upwards in groups, taking advantage of the cover of the

---

12   Things turned out very differently. Some partisans, who had witnessed the retrieval of the money, stated: "When someone asked about the contents of the bags, he [Commandant Costante Federici] replied to some that there were papers, to some others that there was coffee, and to some others again tea, so nothing could be found out". (Angelo Bendotti and Giuliana Bertacchi, *Il difficile cammino della giustizia e della libertà*. Il filo di Arianna, Bergamo, 1983, p. 125). General Masini of the Tito Speri also conducted an investigation into the matter, but it was not possible to recover the money.

rocks and continuing to fire. I then slowly began the chase [...] I was
then urged by the liaison officer to give it up, even if the rebels could be
clearly seen crouching towards the top [...].[13]

The following day, after the hard suffered round-up, Cadorna received a message from the Green Flames of Camonica Valley, where he was invited to reach the village of Darfo Boario Terme, to join a meeting with the various leaders of this formation, probably in Villa Cemmi.[14] The General reached his destination the following day, travelling on a bus. Everything went smoothly, his unkempt appearance of a man in his fifties did not arouse any suspicion, moreover, being the eve of the 15th August (The religious Italian holiday called Ferragosto), the climate was very festive and even the German soldiers seemed to enjoy the long sunny days. It was only between the Cavallina Valley and the Camonica Valley that Cadorna was suddenly brought back to harsh reality, when he spotted several roadside signs reading: "Achtung! Banditen!". Reached the town of Darfo, he found it well guarded by the Germans, as the Waffenschule Oberbefehlshaber Südwest, a weapons school for Wehrmacht officer trainees, had been installed here since June 1944. He immediately met General Masini and Alpine Captain Romolo Ragnoli, leaders of the local Green Flames, who explained him the general situation: the bottom of the valley was firmly occupied by the Germans, who were interested in the Camonica Valley as a possible escape route to Alto Adige and then Austria, while the side valleys and the mountains were completely under the control of the partisans. The partisans had managed, with various coups, to recover weapons and ammunition and also had an excellent logistical organisation, which

---

13   My translation.
14   Don Carlo Comensoli writes in his diary: "13/08/1944: Today, from Milan, an
     urgent message brought by a young man from Bonicelli: we have found the
     device (it must be our radio) and we must take urgent action. At Camp No. 3,
     4 Englishmen have come, they want a meeting with the Commander. He
     leaves immediately. It is now 11 p.m. and he still hasn't returned." Don Carlo
     believes that the four members of the mission are all English, he had evidently
     been misinformed. The only Englishman present was Churchill. By
     "Commander", he means Captain Romolo Ragnoli, who would actually meet
     Cadorna in Darfo in the following days.

allowed transfers and connections with Switzerland, thanks to their own units also located in Valtellina territory.

After the meeting, the General came back and reached Ranzanico again on 16ᵗʰ August, where he found his camp on high alert. Word of his presence in the area had spread. To avoid further risks, Cadorna decided to move to Milan together with De Laurentiis, having understood the impossibility of establishing his base in Camonica Valley. He then ordered Churchill and radio operator Delle Monache to reach the various groups of the Green Flames in the Valley, while remaining in constant contact with Milan, thanks to a courier from the local formations. The task assigned by the General was to act, by radio and with the help of relays, as a communication link with the Allied Command, to understand the needs of the local partisans and, where possible, to prepare possible landing fields for future deliveries of materials and armaments. When he arrived in Milan, Cadorna established his base and came into contact with various leading exponents of the Organizzazione Franchi, the CLNAI and the CVL, including Ferruccio Parri.

Churchill and Delle Monache remained in the valley for about a month, but nothing, not even in the official reports, was written down or reported about this period, only small unimportant hints. So, I began researching various local history books trying to find clues about the inter-allied mission in the Camonica Valley. In addition, I also tried to find still living testimonies, hoping to collect as much details as possible.

Churchill and Delle Monache began the difficult journey from Ranzanico to the Camonica Valley. Like Cadorna, however, the English Major had a very bad parachute landing, so much so that he could hardly walk. When he landed on some rocks, he seriously injured his leg and his long march was very difficult and tiring. He moved on foot, together with his companion, almost at night and along difficult and little-trodden paths. From Ranzanico he reached the farmstead called Malga Lunga, on the mountains between the villages of Sovere and Gandino, at an altitude of 1,235 metres above sea level, which was the main refuge of the 53ʳᵈ Garibaldi partisan brigade, later known as the "13 martyrs of Lovere" and then, perhaps on 18ᵗʰ August, the Camonica Valley. Here, he surely met Don Carlo

Comensoli (a priest who was one of the main leaders of the Green Flames Groups) although there is no mention of this meeting in his diary. However, the spiritual commander of the Green Flames was certainly aware of this Allied mission as he mentioned it more than once in his writings.[15] Churchill and his companions tried in vain to track down group C3 of Green Flames, located in the upper Valgrigna (a small valley adjacent to Camonica Valley) but on 18th August, the day of their arrival, the Germans were carrying out a violent round-up in that area. A few days earlier, in fact, two German soldiers fell into an ambush on the mountains of the small village of Esine, in a place called Fontanì de l'Aligrìna, set by the same group C3 (and assisted by C1). In retaliation for this tragic action, the Germans carried out a large-scale round-up, burning almost all the farmhouses in the mountain areas. Once again, and within a week, Churchill and Delle Monache found themselves in the middle of a round-up and for a while they had to remain hidden.

Thanks to the testimony of Salvina and Giuseppina Gelfi, two old ladies who were respectively born in 1927 and 1919 and lived in Esine at that time, Churchill's presence was verified. The old sisters told me that their family gave hospitality, in their farmstead, to an English officer who had parachuted a few days before. They also added that, more than once, they were forced to hide him under piles of hay, because their farmhouse was repeatedly ransacked by the Germans who, at that time, August 1944, were always searching for partisans. Among the many details mentioned by the two sisters, some caught my attention more than the others. According to their recollections, the British officer was limping and had a leg severely wounded, which was lovingly treated by the sisters and their mother. In recognition of his hospitality, the Englishman also gave to the Gelfi family his own parachute, later used to tailor new clothes in silk. All these were clues which confirmed the Churchill's presence at the Gelfi farmstead on the mountains of Esine, at an altitude of

---

15   Don Carlo Comensoli's diary reads: "19.8.44: Clandestine messages arrived today: For General Cadorna et Major *Peters*. Very pleased to hear that you have arrived well, stop. Please start connection at earliest possible time. If any difficulties communicate through this radio, stop. Inform us what are your plans for the division". (p. 193, vol. 3).

1.389 metres above sea level, at the end of August 1944. Salvina and Giuseppina also told me that Churchill, before leaving, wrote a long letter which he gave to their old father. In Italian, he wrote in great detail that he had been greatly helped by the Gelfi family and then asked them to hide the important document. It would have been useful for the family only after a future liberation by the Allies, to get a reward for the help given to him. However, according to what the two daughters told me, the family burned the letter after short time, since the Germans used to search their old farm house every now and then. Churchill remained with the two sisters for about a week and, after recovering and waiting for the end of the German roundup, left the farmhouse.[16] He then tried, together with Delle Monache and not without difficulty, to reach group C3 of the Green Flames, but the movements of a British officer were obviously very dangerous, also considering the fact that the only cover he had, in case he was stopped by the Germans or the Fascist authorities, was a false identity card and a not very credible Italian accent.[17]

In the mountains of the village of Bienno, the two finally managed to find the Captain of the local Green Flames group C3 *Sandro*,[18] who was very enthusiastic about their arrival. In the book *Lionello Levi Sandri - Una vita per la libertà e la giustizia* (Lionello Levi Sandri - A life for freedom and justice), we can read a report written by *Sandro* himself about the arrival of the English officer, his radio operator and the various attempts to make the radio work:

> *27 August. The device (the radio) can be set up quite comfortably up here. A small modification is needed and we hope to be able to do it today so that it will work tomorrow... 29 August. The device is set*

---

16 The radio operator was never mentioned by the Gelfi sisters, and the two probably separated for a while because of the large-scale round-up, in order not to be too conspicuous and to arouse suspicion among the population. What Delle Monache did is not known.

17 According to this document, he appeared to be employed in an electricity company in the Valley, whose headquarters were in Milan, although this cover was not supported by any contact in the same company.

18 Lionello R. Levi Sandri (Milan, 5 October 1910 - Rome, 11 April 1991) was an Italian jurist, partisan, anti-fascist and magistrate. A socialist statesman, he was a European Commissioner, Councillor and President of the Council of State.

up nicely and will be able to start regular service from tonight. I think that in the event of a roundup it might be useful to call for Allied air support. We could find possible road and rail targets to be bombed, so as to interdict operations considerably....

Between 29th August and 3rd September, Churchill visited the various partisan groups in the area with Captain *Sandro*, who continued as follows:

We returned last night after visiting C4, C5, C3, C1. Our friend (Churchill) was partially satisfied, and partially he noticed some deficiencies. He is a thorough and fussy guy. We also had a look at the launch site at Malga Frà, which he found in a good position and perfectly suited to the purpose. But regarding its use, he did not give us much hope at the moment.

The partisan Vitale Bonettini (*Tani*) of the group C3, in his diary, notes Churchill's presence in those very days, confirming and adding some details about the trip that took them to Malga Frà, on the mountains of Esine, an area considered suitable for possible future parachute jumps:

One beautiful day, Captain Sandro arrives with a man calling himself Mr. Antonio. I notice that he shouldn't be one of us, he is well groomed and too clean. Somebody says he is an English Major. As scouts, Cico and I accompany him with the Captain and his brother Libero to the launch site. [...] The same day, or maybe the day after (I think it was the 2nd September 1944), I accompanied him, again with Captain Sandro, to Lieutenant Silvio's camp on the mountains of Esine, about four hours' march away; with us, instead of Cico, was Vittorino.

Giulio Mazzon (*Silvio*), Commander of the group C1, writes in his book *"C1 "Silvio" Vallecamonica - Nella Resistenza Bresciana* (*"C1 Silvio" – Vallecamonica – In the Resistance of Brescia*):

After the round-up on Esine's mountains, a certain Major Antonio came to visit me, impeccably dressed in bourgeois clothes. He was an Englishman who wandered around, inspecting the groups of the Green Flames. Later I was told that his name was Peter Churchill. (Note again the confusion of the name which is one more time reported incorrectly).

I had a valuable guest, but it was at great risk too. Our conversations were sloppy, made up of English and Italian words or carried thanks to little drawings on slips of paper. He asked to play chess. It was easy for him to win the games. He was able to assess the efficiency of the C1 and appreciated the self-sacrifice of the patrols in the rain.

After these initial patrols, Churchill and Delle Monache tried to make the radio work. Unfortunately, perhaps due to damage during the parachute jump or other technical problems, they were never able to use the equipment properly. In addition, the Major started to have some problems with his radio operator, whom he considered not very bright, not very brave and not suitable for his role. So, he began to collaborate assiduously with Andrea Pedretti (*Andreino*), born in 1921, a radio telegrapher enlisted as a partisan in *Libero*'s C3 and who worked alongside him throughout the period spent on the mountains. They too managed to accomplish very little. The same *Andreino*, however, during an interview with me in the Autumn of 2012, confessed with great satisfaction that, with the collaboration of Churchill and thanks to another radio device, they were able to make the Allied Air Force bomb some local train convoys loaded with food and ammunition destined for the German Command of the Waffenschule Oberbefehlshaber Südwest installed in Boario Terme.

However, Churchill and Delle Monache's task, indicated by General Cadorna, could no longer be carried out, as the means at their disposal were unusable. Establishing a link between the local partisan Commands of the Green Flames and the Allies, for future launches of food, weapons and supplies, without a fully functioning radio, resulted almost impossible.

So, on 14th September, Churchill and Delle Monache decided to reach Cadorna and the Organizzazione Franchi, a Badoglian military formation led by Edoardo Sogno. So reported Cadorna in his book *La Riscossa*:

Major Churchill was soon fed up with that alpine hermitage, and with Sogno's connivance, he descended to the plain and settled in Villa Casana at Novedrate, not far from Milan.

The officer remained here for about two and a half months, undertaking, among other things, a number of trips to Turin and Biella, where he was able to collaborate with another Allied Special Force mission, *Cherokee Mission*, led by Major Alistair MacDonald. General Cadorna in his book wrote:

> *But his position as liaison officer was compromised by the fact that he did not have an efficient radio station. Since I, like him, felt the need to inform the Allies of the real state of the situation in Upper Italy, I could only warmly approve Churchill's intention to return to Liberated Italy via Switzerland.*

When, on 2nd December, after being informed that his position had become precarious, Churchill took a train to Como, under the pseudonym of Giulio Kravic (Italian-Slovene name to explain his foreign accent in case of need). From here, it was easy for him to cross the Swiss border on foot. Firstly, he reached Lugano, then Geneva and finally Bern, where he met John McCaffery, head of the Italian section of the SOE installed in the Swiss capital. After a few days, he entered France and reached Marseilles, where he flew back to the SOE headquarters near Brindisi. It was not until 27th January that he was able to return to England and write a detailed report on the recently concluded *Operation Floodlight/Fairway*. On the same day, he was awarded the *Distinguished Service Order* medal:

> *This officer was parachuted into N. Italy on 12 Aug 44 to act as head of the British Liaison Mission to the command of the Partisan Movement in Northern Italy. Since this date he has been Chief Liaison Officer to the C.L.N.A.I. and to the Partisan Central Command, both tasks of great responsibility. During the entire period under review he has shown outstanding ability, considerable initiative, and has at all times been reliable in his information. Captain Churchill is head of our most important mission.*
> *—Lieutenant Colonel Richard Thornton Hewitt,*
> *Commanding Officer of the Allied No 1 Special Force in the Italian Campaign.*[19]

19   *The National Archives*, Kew (UK) – Ref. n. HS 9/316/3.

In the spring of 1945, Churchill returned to Italy for a short mission, only to come back to England on 6th May, when the war was over. On 7th July, he officially ended his career in the Special Operations Executive, which was officially disbanded on 16th January 1946, exactly five and a half years after its creation. The *Fairway* Mission certainly wasn't very productive for the partisans of the Camonica Valley and, according to Churchill, the whole thing was compromised by the broken radio. Communications with Cadorna himself in Milan were frighteningly slow. It took about 7 days for a message to be delivered by a courier and this was the main reason why he moved from the Valley to Milan. His job as liaison officer was practically useless with that timing. It must also be said that, apart from the bombing of the German convoy, there are no other evident results of his stay in the Valley, also considering the fact that nothing was ever dropped in the landing field located at Malga Frà on the mountains of Esine.

In his report on this mission, Churchill mostly described all the details, characters and particulars of his stay in the Milan area with General Cadorna and the Franchi Organisation. He also wrote a few interesting words on the Green Flames of the Camonica Valley:

> *The group of the Fiamme Verdi, known as the South Camonica Brigade, numbered about 300 well-disciplined men and boys, led by a group of zealous and regular Alpini chosen for their leadership qualities and their knowledge of mountain warfare. Each of the Brigade's small bands of 30 men also had two or three Russians as well as a German deserter. The food was good and plentiful, if unvarying, and every day they had home-killed meat, polenta and milk. Everything was paid for with Green Flame coupons, to be redeemed after the war. As all Green Flames are natives of the area and do not indulge in looting, they get all the help they needed, and more, from the valley dwellers.*

After the war, Oliver returned to and established in Cambridge. Here he married Ruth Briggs,[20] a key member of the British

---

20   Audrey Ruth Briggs (1920 - June 2005) graduated in Modern Languages to Newnham College, Cambridge. From 1942-1945, she worked, as an expert in German, at Bletchley Park as a member of the Z Watch, which translated the decrypted messages. She worked variously in Huts 4 and 5, Block A (N), and

Intelligence crypto-analysis team at Bletchley Park during the war, and had three children.

Figure 9. Wedding of Oliver and Ruth in 1948 at Worcester Cathedral where her father was a Canon. Her wedding dress was made from parachute silk.

Pierluigi Tumiati, a leading member of the Italian Resistance in World War II, visited them in Cambridge in 1946 and was the first person in their visitor book which created after their marriage. In his SOE Personal File, Oliver makes a number of references to him, who was head of the Milan Franchi Organisation and accompanied him to safety in Switzerland when he had to leave Italy in a hurry in December 1944.

Naval Section NS I - German Cryptography. Briggs's work has been recognised in breaking codes used by the Axis powers during the war.

Oliver worked as an architect in Cambridge until his death in 1997, at the age of 83.

In September 2012, her son Simon was my guest in Camonica Valley. Together with him, we went to the same places where his father worked during the war and we were able to have a meeting with a very emotional Andrea Pedretti (*Andreino*), the Italian radio operator of the group C3, who was always at the side of the mysterious *Mr. Antonio* between August and September 1944 in the Camonica Valley.[21]

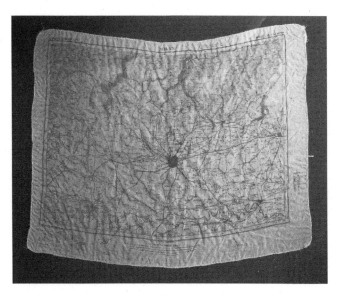

Figure 10. Oliver Churchill's silk escape map of Milan area during the war. Silk had advantages over paper for a number of reasons: it was waterproof, fairly indestructible, made no sound when being unfolded or folded, felt like a handkerchief if the person was frisked, and could be quickly and silently swallowed to avoid detection. This map is property of Simon Churchill, Oliver's son.

---

21 *Andreino*'s opinion of Churchill and his actions was very positive, as were those of General Cadorna, Lionello Levi Sandri and Giulio Mazzon. According to others, however, he was at least an ambiguous character. P. Secchia - F. Frassati, *La Resistenza e gli Alleati (The Resistance and the Allies)*, Feltrinelli, Milan, 1962, p. 143: "a singular character, whom the N. 1 Special Force, with an unfortunate hand, had placed alongside General Cadorna". Max Salvadori, *Resistenza ed azione*, Laterza, Bari, 1951, p. 257: "an officer as brave as short of brain".

10.5 *Ice hockey*

Walter, Peter, and Oliver were encouraged to take up ice-skating by their mother who was a proficient figure skater. Peter was extremely proficient at ice hockey, playing in the Cambridge University ice hockey team which he captained in his final year, and winning 15 international caps. Walter also played at international level. In those days there were very limited facilities in England to learn to skate and to practice ice hockey, and so it was difficult to become as proficient as players in northern Europe and in countries like Canada and the US, where ice rinks were plentiful and the sport well established. Since there was no ice rink in Cambridge, while he was at university Peter had to travel 100 km to London to practice.

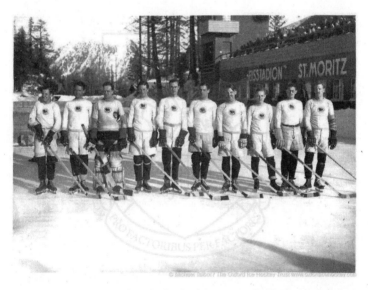

Figure 11. Cambridge University ice hockey team at St Moritz, Switzerland, in January 1931. Peter is second from right.

Figure 12. England *vs* Canada, 20th January 1932.
Walter and Peter are kneeling at the front.

Figure 13. Oliver playing ice hockey, but the teams and the location are unknown.
He is the man in the left in the foreground.

10.6 *Memorial to the three Churchill brothers*

This short paragraph demonstrates how extraordinary the history of the Churchill family is, especially that of the three brothers Walter, Peter and Oliver who, with their participation and contribution to the Second War, left us an invaluable heritage.

After Coventry had been heavily bombed in 1941, Walter Churchill moved his engineering company from Coventry to Market Bosworth, where it has remained ever since. After the Market Bosworth Historical Society became aware of the wartime gallantry of not just Walter, but also of Peter and Oliver, it decided to fund a Memorial Cairn.

Figure 14. Inauguration of the Churchill brothers' Memorial. James and Andrew Churchill (respectively son and grandson of Walter) are the second and the third form right. In the next page (Figures 15, 16, 17, 18) all the four faces of the granite Cairn, dedicated to the three brothers and to all the Churchill Staff of the JJ Churchill Ltd.

The granite Cairn is located in front of the JJ Churchill factory, and was unveiled in autumn 2015. Three of the four sides commemorate each of the Churchill brothers, while the fourth side commemorates the factory's relocation from Coventry to Market Bosworth and Walter landing his Hurricane in the field opposite, while overseeing the factory's move.

AKNOWLEDGMENTS

First of all, I want to thank Ms. Rosalie Spire, archivist in The National Archives in Kew (UK), who helped me with the confusion over Peter and Oliver's *noms-de-guerre*. Without her initial help, it would have been very difficult for me to find out the key to the problem with all the similar war names the two secret agent brothers chose for their missions.

My gratitude then goes to Amyas Crump, who introduced me to Sophie Parker, granddaughter of Odette. Thanks to this contact and to Sophie's willingness, I was able to collect information and documents about Peter and his wife unpublished before and put them in my book.

I am very grateful to Simon Churchill who, over the last years, has encouraged me in the research about his uncles, father, and all his extraordinary ancestors. Since I found him after a long research, we have constantly kept in touch and we have met several times; I was guest in his house and he in mine, and in this way I was able to meet a wonderful person who became a true friend in life.

My special thanks go to my old friend Massimo Squaratti for the work done with the cover of this book.

I must say thank you also to Professor Valentina Adami of the University of Verona for her kindness and assistance during the drafting of my work and, finally, to Professor David Stafford, a giant in the historical research, who honoured me in writing the preface of this book, making it more valuable.

BIBLIOGRAPHY

Adami V., *Trauma studies and Literature – Martin Amis's Time's Arrow as Trauma Fiction*, Peter Lang GmbH Internationaler Verlag der Wissenschaften, Frankfurt am Main, 2008.

Anni R. – Botteri I., *Il diario originale e inedito di Carlo Comensoli (18 ottobre 1943 – 24marzo 1945)*, Archivio storico della Resistenza Bresciana e dell'età contemporanea, Brescia, 2007.

Attridge J., "Two Types of Secret Agency: Conrad, Causation, and Popular Spy Fiction", University of Texas Press, *Texas Studies in Literature and language*, Vol. 55, Nr. 2, Summer 2013, pp. 125-158.

Balaev M., "Trends in Literary Trauma Theory", in *Mosaic: An Interdisciplinary Critical Journal*, Vol. 41, Nr. 2, June 2008, pp. 149-166.

Beecham R. G., "Fiction and memoir of Britain's Great War: disillusioned or disparate?", European Review of History: Revue européenne d'histoire, 2015, pp. 791-813.

Bendotti A. – Bertacchi G., *Il difficile cammino della giustizia e della libertà*, Il filo di Arianna, Bergamo, 1983.

Bolton J., "Mid-Term Autobiography and the Second World War", *Journal of Modern Literature*, vol. 30, no. 1, 2006, pp. 155-172.

Bonettini V., *La neve cade sui monti – Dal diario di un ribelle*, El Caròbe, Esine, 1975.

Brittain V., *Testament of Youth: An Autobiographical Study of the Years 1900-1925*, London, Virago, 1983.

Cadorna Jr. R., *La Riscossa: La testimonianza del generale dei partigiani con documenti inediti,* Bietti, Milano, 1977.

Caruth C., *Unclaimed Experience: Trauma, Narrative, and History*, Baltimore, MD: Johns Hopkins UP, 1996.

Churchill P., *All About the French Riviera*, Vista Books, 1960.

Churchill P., *By Moonlight*, Robert Hale Limited, London, 1958.

Churchill P., *Duel of Wits*, Hodder and Stoughton, London, 1953.

Churchill P., *Of Their Own Choice*, Hodder and Stoughton, London, 1952.

Churchill P., *The Spirit in the Cage*, Hodder and Stoughton, London, 1954.

Churchill W. A., *Watermarks in paper in Holland, England, France, etc. in the XVII and XVIII centuries and their interconnection*, De Graaf, 1935.

Cobley E., "Description in Realist Discourse: The War Novel." *Style*, vol. 20, no. 3, 1986, pp. 395-410.

Cominini A., "La missione alleata Fairway: Un Churchill in Valle Camonica", in *Gli Alleati a Brescia tra guerra e ricostruzione – Fonti, ricerche, interpretazioni*, edited by Rolando Anni, Giovanni Gregorini, Maria Paola Pasini, Franco Angeli Edizioni, Milano, 2018, pp.135-154.

Cominini A., "La ricerca di Katarina", in *Studi e ricerche di storia contemporanea n. 83-84*, Anno 44°, Istituto Bergamasco per la storia della Resistenza e dell'età contemporanea, Bergamo, giugno-dicembre 2015, pp. 74-82.

Cziborra P., *KZ Wolkenburg: Todesmarsch nach Dachau (Die Außenlager des KZ Flossenbürg)*, Lorbeer-Verlag, June 2018.

De Man P., "The Resistance to Theory", *Theory and History of Literature*, Volume 33, University of Minnesota Press, Minneapolis, London, 1986, p. 11.

Derwin S., "Reviewed Work(s): The Belated Witness: Literature, Testimony and the Question of Holocaust Survival by Michael Levine", The Johns Hopkins University Press, *MLN*, Vol. 123, Nr. 5, Comparative Literature Issue, Dec. 2008, pp. 1191-1194.

Drabble M., *Spy fiction*, from *The Concise Oxford Companion to English Literature*, Stringer, Jenny, Hahn, Daniel (eds), Oxford University Press, Oxford, 2007.

Falchi G., *Lionello Levi Sandri. Una vita per la libertà e la giustizia,* I quaderni di La Resistenza Bresciana – n. 5, Archivio Storico della Resistenza Bresciana e dell'età contemporanea, Brescia, October 1992.

Felman S., "Education and Crisis, or the Vicissitudes of Teaching", in C. Caruth (ed.), *Trauma: Explorations in Memory*, p. 15.

Felman S., "In an Era of Testimony: Claude Lanzmann's *Shoah*", Yale French Studies 97, 2000, pp. 105-106.

Fitzpatrick S., "Writing History/Writing about Yourself: What's the Difference?" *Clio's Lives: Biographies and Autobiographies of Historians*, Doug Munro and John G. Reid, ANU Press, Australia, 2017, pp. 17-38.

Foot M. R. D., S*OE in France. An Account of the Work of the British Special Operations Executive in France 1940–1944*, London: H. M. Stationery Office, 1966.

Graves R., *Good-Bye to All That*, Harmondsworth, Penguin, 1960.

Hartman G., *The Longest Shadow*, Indiana University Press, 1996.

Hemingway E., *A Farewell to Arms,* Charles Scribner's Sons, New York, 1929.

Iser W., *The Act of Reading: A Theory of Aesthetic Response*, The John Hopkins University Press, London, 1971.

Isherwood I. A., *Remembering the Great War. Writing and publishing the experiences of World War I*, I.B.Tauris, 28 feb. 2017, Chapter I.

Klinkowitz J., "New Journalism and the nonfiction novel", from *Encyclopedia of the Novel,* Schellinger, Paul (ed.); Hudson, Christopher; Rijsberman, Marijke (asst eds), Chicago; London: Fitzroy Dearborn Publishers, 1998, 2 vols.

Kramer R., *Flames in the Field: The Story of Four SOE Agents in Occupied France*, Michael Joseph Ltd, 1995.

Marks L., *Between Silk and Cyanide: A Code Maker's War 1941–45*, published September 12th 2000 by Free Press, 1998.

Mars A., *Unbroken. The True Story of a Submarine*, Pan Books, London, 1954.

Mazzon G., *C1 "Silvio" Vallecamonica. Nella Resistenza Bresciana*, Arti grafiche Jasillo, Roma,1997.

Miller N. and Tougaw J., "Introduction: Extremities", in N. Miller and J. Tougaw, eds. *Extremities*, p. 2.

Montgomery B. L., *The Memoirs of Field-Marshal the Viscount Montgomery of Alamein*, Collins, London, 1958.

Mostafa D. S., "Literary Representations of Trauma, Memory, and Identity in the Novels of Elias Khoury and Rabī Jābir", Brill, Journal of Arabic Literature, Vol. 40, No. 2, 2009, pp. 208-236.

Newman B., "Spies in fact and fiction", Journal of the Royal Society of Arts, Vol. 103, No. 4943, 21st January, 1955, pp. 131-133.

Okonjo O. C., "The Poetics of the War Novel", *Comparative Literature Studies*, vol. 20, no. 2, 1983, pp. 203-216.

Olster S., "New Journalism and the Nonfiction Novel", *The Cambridge Companion to American Fiction After 1945*, Duvall John N. (Ed.), New York, 2012, pp. 44-55.

Partsch C., "The case of Richard Sorge: Secret Operations in the German past in 1950s Spy Fiction", University of Wisconsin Press, Monatshefte, Vol. 97, Nr. 4, Winter 2005, pp.628-653.

Richardi H. G., *Ostaggi delle SS al lago di Braies - la deportazione in Alto Adige di illustri prigionieri dei lager nazisti provenienti da 17 paesi europei*, Archivio di Storia Contemporanea, Braies,2006.

Rodwell G., *Defining the Historical Novel*, in *Whose History? - Engaging History Students through Historical Fiction*, University of Adelaide Press, 2013.

Rothberg M., "Between the Extreme and the Everyday", in N. Miller and J. Tougaw, eds., Extremities, p.75.

Salvadori M., *Resistenza ed azione*, Laterza, Bari, 1951.

Saunders M., "Life Writing, Fiction and Modernism in British Narratives of the First World War", The RUSI Journal, 2014, pp. 106-11.

Schmidt S. J. and Hauptmeier H., "The Fiction Is That Reality Exists: A Constructivist Model of Reality, Fiction, and Literature", Poetics Today, Vol. 5, No. 2, *The Construction of Reality in Fiction* 1984, pp. 253-274.

Secchia P. – Frassati F., *La Resistenza e gli Alleati*, Feltrinelli, Milano, 1962.

Sinor J., "Inscribing ordinary trauma in the diary of a military child", University of Hawaii Press, Vol. 26, No. 3, Summer 2003, pp. 405-427.

Slotkin R., *Fiction for the Purposes of History, Rethinking History*, 2005.

Stafford D. A. T., *Spies and Gentlemen: The Birth of the British Spy Novel, 1893-1914*, Indiana University Press, Victorian Studies, Vol. 24, Nr. 4, Summer 1981.

Tickell J., *Odette: the story of a British agent*, Chapman & Hall, London (UK), 1949.

Verdina N. – Bosco Verdina C., *La Resistenza nel Loverese. Documenti, testimonianze e studi,* Comitato per le celebrazioni del XXX della resistenza, Lovere, 1975.

Von Schlabrendorff F. and Von Gaevernitz G., *Offiziere gegen Hitler, nach einem Erlebnisbericht von Fabian v. Schlabrendorff,* Europa Verlag, Zürich, 1946.

Wake P., "Except in the case of historical fact: history and the historical novel", *Rethinking History*, 2016, pp. 80-96.

White H., "Introduction: Historical Fiction, Fictional History, and Historical Reality, Rethinking History", 2005, pp.147-157.

Winks R. W. and McGrew E. G., "Spy Fiction – Spy Reality: From Conrad to Le Carre", Soundings: An Interdisciplinary Journal, Vol. 76, Nr. 2/3, Papers from the Drew Symposium, Summer/Fall 1993, pp. 221-244.

Wolfe T., *The Kandy-Kolored Tangerine-Flake Streamline Baby, Farrar,* Straus and Giroux, New York, 1965.

Zipfel F., "Non-Fiction Novel", from *Routledge Encyclopedia of Narrative Theory,* London: Routledge, 2010.

OTHER RESEARCH TOOLS

The National Archives (TNA) of Kew (UK): http://www.nationalarchives.gov.uk/
The British Pathé Archive: https://www.britishpathe.com/
Archivio storico della Resistenza bresciana e dell'età contemporanea of Brescia (I): https://centridiricerca.unicatt.it/resistenza
ISREC BG - Istituto bergamasco per la storia della Resistenza e dell'età contemporanea of Bergamo (I): http://www.isrecbg.it/web/
Private Archives of Churchill's descendants
Marie Baud's Archive from www.aerosteles.net
The London Gazette

INDEX

For obvious reasons, in the following index of names, that of Peter Churchill has been omitted, together with all his noms-de-guerre.

MIMESIS GROUP
www.mimesis-group.com

MIMESIS INTERNATIONAL
www.mimesisinternational.com
info@mimesisinternational.com

MIMESIS EDIZIONI
www.mimesisedizioni.it
mimesis@mimesisedizioni.it

ÉDITIONS MIMÉSIS
www.editionsmimesis.fr
info@editionsmimesis.fr

MIMESIS COMMUNICATION
www.mim-c.net

MIMESIS EU
www.mim-eu.com

Printed by
Puntoweb s.r.l. – Ariccia (RM)
October 2022